TO SAVE AMERICA

How to Prevent Our Coming
Federal Bankruptcy

by Martin L. Buchanan

For the younger generation at The Independence Institute

ISBN-13: 978-1-4196-7330-6

ISBN-10: 1-4196-7330-0

LCCN: 2007905345

Published by BookSurge LLC
www.booksurge.com
866 303 6235, orders@booksurge.com

Manufactured in the United States of America.

About the Author

Martin L. Buchanan lives in Denver, Colorado, where he works for a respected consulting firm by day and writes at night. He is a U.S. Army and Army National Guard veteran.

Dedication

For my wife, who insists that an unbalanced budget is no budget at all.

CONTENTS

List of Figures

List of Tables

1 INTRODUCTION

You need to read this book because our federal government is going broke. As shown in Figure 1.1, federal liabilities have grown 150% in a six year period, from about twenty trillion dollars to about fifty trillion dollars.[1] These liabilities are now more than six hundred thousand dollars per U.S. family.

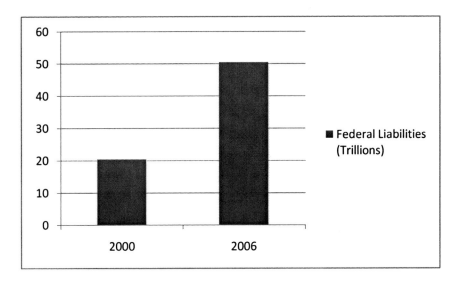

**Figure 1.1 Federal Liabilities
2000 and 2006 ($ Trillions)**

Reading this book will take you a few hours. If you rely on government benefits or contracts, expect to receive Social Security or Medicare, pay taxes, or invest in the USA, then our federal budget crisis and how it is resolved will have a big effect on your future. If you vote, this book should affect what you ask of politicians and how you vote.

The Story of the Great Ship

Imagine all of us on a great ocean liner, the grandest in the world. It cuts through cold seas and blustery winds, providing safety and luxury within its steel hull. In the grand ballroom, men in tuxedos and women in evening gowns waltz to the sounds of a classical orchestra. Young people giggle and sip champagne. Tables are piled with gourmet food. You and your family have been on the voyage for so long that the life boat drill conducted at the trip's beginning is a vague memory.

As the clock nears midnight, you notice crew members and ship's officers moving urgently, talking in hushed tones, heading towards the bridge and the deck. A few passengers also go up to the deck. Through the ship's many levels they feel the rumble of the great engines, propelling them at full speed. There is too much light in the night air, more than the full moon above would provide. Then, to their horror, they see disaster straight ahead of the ship, looming above them just three miles away, a brilliant wall of ice reflecting the moonlight, three hundred feet high and a mile wide. In ten minutes the ship will collide with that giant iceberg.

You and your family are among the lucky few half an hour later, shivering in an overcrowded lifeboat, rowing through icy waves, watching the great ship sink, carrying thousands to watery graves. The bitter crewman guiding your boat tells an incredible story. He says that for the eight hours before the disaster, the captain and officers knew that the iceberg was there. Instead of slowing the ship and steering away from disaster, the captain sped up and steered directly toward it, as if he wished to destroy the great ship.

Why I Wrote This Book

This is not a book about particular politicians, but one politician in particular caused me to write this book. In the year 2000 election, I voted for George W. Bush, believing that he would do a better job than Al Gore of controlling spending and avoiding debt. I was disastrously wrong.

Instead of balancing the budget, President Bush ran huge deficits in every year of his term in office. Necessary security spending after 9/11 explained only a small part of the administration's spending. In the first five of the eight budgets under its control, the George W. Bush administration produced deficits totaling more than 1.5 trillion dollars, an average of 300 billion dollars each year. That size of deficit is $1,000 per year per American, or $4,000 per year per family of four. Each year, in addition to whatever mortgage debt, installment debt, and credit card debt a family struggles with, the U.S. government is piling on another $4,000 of debt that must be repaid with interest by our children and grandchildren.

Looming beyond this immediate national debt of trillions of dollars are potential liabilities of tens of trillions of dollars, the Social Security and Medicare costs of nearly 80 million *baby boomers*, Americans born from 1946 to 1964, who begin retiring in 2008. Social Security and Medicare were created by Democratic Presidents, Franklin Roosevelt and Lyndon Johnson. Members of both parties have expanded these programs, including a major new Medicare drug benefit proposed by President Bush and enacted by both parties in Congress in 2005.

I wrote this book as a concerned citizen, holding no office, not engaged in the professions of policy making or journalism, loving my country and hoping to help avert a coming disaster. *To Save America*, this book's title, is not an overstatement. If we do not deal with the problems described in this book, then our country faces a grim future of much higher taxes, economic stagnation, and possible default on our government's obligations.

The facts described in this book are well known by every Congressman, every federal cabinet officer, and both major political parties. These elites are failing us. I've made this book short and written it in plain language for every citizen. My hope is that it will stir us, as a people, to action.

Now you can understand the story of the ocean liner and the iceberg. The iceberg is the looming and multiplying debt. The captain who has steered toward the iceberg rather than away from it is President Bush. At this point, avoiding the iceberg requires more than changing just our President or which party controls the Congress. We need major changes in our government's programs and policies, like the changes described in this book.

The federal budget crisis is bigger than any political party. This book suggests cuts in programs favored by both Democratic and Republican politicians. Because the George W. Bush administration is currently in power and running large federal deficits, this book criticizes that administration. I voted for George W. Bush in 2000; this book is not written to undermine the administration or the Republican Party.

Why Save a Trillion Dollars Each Year?

This book proposes cutting federal spending by about one trillion dollars each year. If the annual federal deficit is now around $250 billion[2], why should we cut federal spending by four times that much? There are five good reasons:

- Social Security and Medicare costs will multiply the deficit in coming years.

- Not all of the proposed cuts may be enacted. You may read this book and agree with most of it, but not want to cut some particular program. If so, embrace the cuts you agree with and reject the rest. For example, one reviewer disliked five proposals that cut a total of $70 billion, but liked the rest of the book, more than 90% of the cuts.

- An exactly balanced budget often produces a deficit. Every family and every nation encounters unexpected expenses. A budget with a surplus allows for such expenses without creating deficits.

- Budget surpluses can be used to pay down debt held by the public. Ideally we would leave a debt-free country to our grandchildren. Paying down debt reduces the government's large annual interest costs.

- One trillion dollars per year in either spending cuts or new tax revenue is about what the government itself estimates is needed to close the fiscal gap.[3]

The federal budget will soon exceed three trillion dollars. Cutting one trillion dollars from that budget leaves a federal budget of two trillion dollars each year. Such a federal government will still have the largest budget in the world.

Why This Book Only Proposes Spending Cuts

If our government spends more than it receives in taxes, then we could cut spending, raise taxes, or some combination. For example, if there is a long-term *fiscal gap* of one trillion dollars a year, we could cut spending five hundred billion dollars and raise taxes five hundred billion dollars per year.

This book is about solving the federal budget crisis entirely with spending cuts, so that the American people have at least one set of options for how to solve the problem entirely by cutting spending. Many of these cuts are severe, and may cause citizens to prefer tax increases instead. What combination of spending cuts and tax increases we choose is up to us and our elected representatives. Many others will write about the federal budget crisis, some proposing tax increases instead of spending cuts.

We Americans already pay one third of our income in taxes to federal, state, and local governments. We work four months each year, until "Tax Freedom Day" on 30 April, just to pay our taxes.[4] Many of us don't want the government to take any more money than the large amounts it already takes, and would rather cut government spending drastically than pay more in taxes.

This book is also designed to be short and simple, presenting clear choices and information for the ordinary citizen. To write in the same way about taxes, tax policy, and tax reform would take a second book as long as this one.

How This Book's Spending Cuts Were Chosen

This book uses these five rules to identify what to cut:

1. *Don't use small spending cuts as an excuse to make major policy changes.* For example, we may not need a Federal Election Commission but cutting it would save only $50 million per year. The cuts in this book don't affect most federal regulatory agencies and commissions.

2. *Restrain Medicare and Social Security rather than replacing them.* Some policy analysts would like to replace Medicare and Social Security with different programs or eliminate them entirely. This book shows how to cut back these programs to make them sustainable, rather than replacing them, without judging the pros or cons of more radical reform.

3. *Stop subsidizing activities that are not primarily the business of the federal government.* For example, end subsidies for private businesses and for activities that are primarily state or local government responsibilities.

4. *Leave core programs that help the poor.* Programs like food stamps are not major causes of our budget problems and such programs are harder to reform or replace.

5. *Solve the entire problem.* As described in Chapter 5, we need to either cut spending or raise revenue by about one trillion dollars per year to eliminate the long-range problems for the federal budget.

This Book's Structure

Chapters 2 to 5 explain the federal budget, federal debt and deficits, the federal budget crisis, and how the federal government may go bankrupt. Chapters 6 to 10 explain the five major ways in which we can save a total of one trillion dollars each year; chapter 11 describes the consequences of these changes, including paying off much of our national debt; and chapter 12 explains how to make fiscal discipline permanent. Appendix A summarizes the proposed spending cuts; Appendix B lists resources for learning more; and Appendix C contains notes on sources.

Beyond Passivity

"Well doctor, what have we got, a republic or a monarchy?"
(asked of Benjamin Franklin)
"A republic, if you can keep it."—Benjamin Franklin

Americans are not passive when attacked by outsiders. After the attacks on Pearl Harbor in 1941 and the World Trade Center in 2001, we vigorously rallied to action. Why should we be passive when a greater threat comes from our own government? That threat is here and real. If our government goes bankrupt, what government will replace it?

This book is being published about one year before the 2008 general election. After you read it, let your Congressional and Presidential candidates know how you want our government to deal with these problems.

Sources and Acknowledgments

Many others have been sounding the alarm about the federal budget crisis for years, notably David M. Walker, Comptroller General of the United States and head of the Government Accountability Office (GAO). This book has also been helped by the work of Peter G. Peterson (author of *Running on Empty* and a founder of the Concord Coalition), by numerous policy studies from the Cato Institute (notably their book *Downsizing the Federal Government* by Chris Edwards), and especially by the book *The Coming Generational Storm* by Laurence J. Kotlikoff and Scott Burns. Publications from America's actuaries, including the American Academy of Actuaries, have been very helpful.

Most of the information in this book comes directly from the federal government, the *Budget of the United States Government, Fiscal Year 2008*, the 2007 trustees' reports for Medicare and Social Security, the *2006 Financial Report of the U.S. Government*, and documents from the GAO, Congressional Budget Office, and Congressional Research Service, all available on the Internet.

Thanks to my father, Dan Karlan, Loretta Czap, and other friends for reviewing drafts of the manuscript. Thanks most of all to my wife, who gave up our evenings and weekends for six months while I wrote this book.

This book and any shortcomings are my responsibilities. No endorsement by any listed authors or institutions, nor by my employer, nor by any reviewers is implied.

2 UNDERSTANDING THE FEDERAL BUDGET

"If the government is big enough to give you everything you want, it is big enough to take away everything you have."
—*President Gerald Ford*

Our government, formed in a rebellion against big government, is now the world's biggest. The U.S. federal government spent $2.6 trillion in fiscal year 2006. Astronomer and author Carl Sagan often spoke of "billions and billions" when describing the numbers of stars and galaxies. Our government now spends trillions and trillions, even larger numbers. The first step in understanding the federal budget is to understand big numbers.

Understanding Big Numbers

"A billion here, a billion there, and pretty soon you're talking about real money."
—*attributed to Senator Everett McKinley Dirksen*

A billion dollars is the smallest amount usually discussed in the federal budget. The total federal budget is approaching three trillion dollars a year. Such large numbers cause many citizens to ignore federal budget discussions, because we are more comfortable with ten dollars, a hundred dollars, or a few thousand dollars, numbers that we deal with personally. We might pay twenty thousand dollars for a car or two hundred thousand dollars for a house. Few Americans ever deal with a sum of one million dollars.

A million dollars is a thousand thousand dollars. A billion dollars is a thousand million dollars. A trillion dollars is a thousand billion dollars.

To put these large numbers in terms that we can all understand, every proposal recommended in this book has a table like the one below. This table shows you how much a proposal will save per person, per family, and for our entire country. It also shows savings each year and the amount saved in a lifetime.

Enact This Book's Proposed Spending Cuts Savings

	Saved Each Year	Saved in a Lifetime
Per Person	$3,865	$309,200
Per Family	$15,460	$1,236,800
For Our Country	$1,159.6 billion	$92,768 billion

To calculate a table like this one, this book uses actual federal spending in fiscal year 2006 (FY 2006), from 10/1/2005 to 9/30/2006, the most recent actual data available. The amount saved each year for our country is rounded to the nearest tenth of a billion dollars. That amount is divided by 300 million Americans to determine the amount saved per person, rounded to the nearest dollar. Per person savings are multiplied by four to determine the amount saved per family. If your family is smaller or larger than four people, adjust accordingly. All of the amounts saved per year are multiplied by 80 to get the amounts saved in a person's lifetime; a typical American lives 80 years.

For example, enacting all of this book's proposals would save the average family more than $15,000 per year and more than one million dollars in a lifetime. These savings may not be in the form of tax cuts, but through avoiding higher taxes, avoiding government bankruptcy, paying down government debt, and leaving our grandchildren a sustainable nation.

Most of the proposed cuts can be made immediately. Some proposals, such as changes in Social Security, produce long-term savings, clearly described as such, and are represented by an equivalent annual amount. This book proposes more than $700 billion per year in immediate savings and more than $400 billion per year in long-term savings.

Budget Talk

Congress enacts *budget authority*, the authorization to spend money. The government then spends money, called *outlays*. The government operates on a *fiscal year (FY)* beginning 1 October of the previous year and lasting through 30 September. For example, FY 2006 was from 1 October 2005 to 30 September 2006. The President's recommended budget for FY 2008 was released in February 2007 and describes all of the actual outlays for FY 2006 used in this book. The President recommends a budget and various supplemental appropriations, but Congress adopts spending (appropriations) bills that may differ.

When outlays exceed revenues, the government has a deficit, which adds to outstanding federal debt. When outlays are less than revenues, the government has a surplus and pays down some of its outstanding debt. Some government debt is held by the public and some is held by the government itself, in trust funds for Social Security and certain other programs.

Some federal spending, such as Social Security retirement payments, is required by laws that don't normally change from year to year; this spending is called *mandatory*. Other spending, which changes more readily from year to year, is called *discretionary*.

The value of our dollar unfortunately changes from year to year, usually decreasing. Comparisons that use *real* dollars are adjusted for inflation so that all figures are converted to dollars for the same year, for a particular comparison.

Some data about federal spending shows spending as a percentage of *gross domestic product (GDP)*. GDP is our nation's total annual economic output, more than thirteen trillion dollars per year in 2006.

This book focuses on cutting actual spending (outlays), whether mandatory or discretionary. Savings are calculated for FY 2006; the dollar amounts saved will be greater in future years.

How Big Is Federal Spending?

In FY 2006, our federal government spent $2,655,435,000,000[5], more than $2.6 trillion.

What Our Federal Government Costs
(Based on FY 2006 Actual Spending)

	Cost Each Year	Cost Over a Lifetime
Per Person	$8,850	$708,000
Per Family	$35,400	$2,832,000
For Our Country	$2,655 billion	$212,400 billion
These are direct federal costs, not including regulatory costs, compliance costs, and tax disincentive costs imposed by the federal government nor the costs of state and local government taxes and regulations.		

So our federal government will cost the average family of four more than $2.8 million over an eighty-year lifetime. Perhaps your family earned only $25,000 last year, paying no federal income taxes and paying a few thousand dollars in payroll taxes. Your costs are less than these averages. A husband and wife working in professional jobs may have earned $200,000 last year, paying high federal income taxes, with costs higher than these averages.

For all of us, what we pay in federal payroll taxes and income taxes is just part of the federal cost burden. The government also takes payroll taxes and corporate income taxes from our employers, money that would otherwise go to workers, stockholders, or customers. As we'll see in Chapter 3, our government also borrows some of what it spends, borrowed money that must be repaid with interest in the future, by us or by our children and grandchildren.

Another way economists look at federal spending is as a percentage of GDP, our country's total economic output. FY 2006 GDP was $13,061.1 billion[6] and federal spending was 20.3% of GDP, a typical federal share in recent years.

Where the Money Goes

Table 2.1 shows where the money went in FY 2006.

Table 2.1. Federal Spending by Category[7]

Category	Spending Amount	Percentage
Military and veterans	$592 billion	22%
Old Age and Survivors Insurance (OASI)	$454 billion	17%
Medicare	$330 billion	12%
Medicaid and related	$186 billion	7%
Net interest	$227 billion	9%
Other	$866 billion	33%

This first look at federal spending shows that five spending categories consume two thirds of the federal budget, that we are spending heavily on our military, even more heavily on benefits for retirees (OASI and Medicare, approaching one third of the entire budget), and that health care spending on Medicare and Medicaid is a large part of the federal budget.

Federal Spending Trends

Figure 2.1 shows annual federal spending at ten-year intervals over the last fifty years.[8]

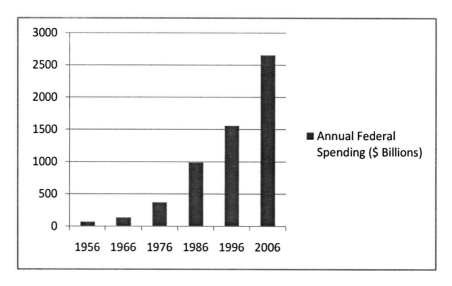

Figure 2.1. Federal Spending 1956-2006 ($ Billions)

Figure 2.1 also shows the most effective way to lie with numbers, by telling the truth. Federal spending in 2006 was more than 37 times greater than spending in 1956, an average growth rate of 7.5% per year, with spending more than doubling every ten years.

These truthful figures are misleading for three reasons. First, the value of the dollar drops. It took $7.41 in 2006 to buy what $1.00 bought in 1956. Second, population increases, so that government spending increases even if spending per person is the same. U.S. population grew from 169 million in 1956 to 300 million in 2006. Third, productivity and real wages typically grow, so government can also grow without increasing its share of the economy.

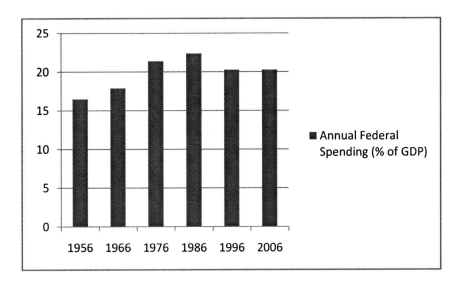

Figure 2.2. Federal Spending 1956-2006 (% of GDP)

Figure 2.2 shows a clearer way to look at federal spending trends, as a share of GDP. Federal spending as a share of economic output is not growing, but is the same (20.3% of GDP) in 2006 as in 1996, and is lower than the 22.4% of GDP that federal spending consumed in 1986.[9]

Based on Figure 2.2, you could conclude that there is no federal budget crisis. Chapter 3 examines our large federal debt and deficits, and whether our growing debt will produce a federal budget crisis.

3 UNDERSTANDING FEDERAL DEBT AND DEFICITS

"I don't have any experience in running up a $4 trillion debt."–H. Ross Perot, 1992 Presidential candidate, responding to President George H. W. Bush's emphasis on the value of governmental experience

Perhaps you have good credit. If so you probably receive several letters a month offering to loan you money. You may have a mortgage, a car payment, and a credit card balance, but as long as you have good credit you can borrow more money when you need it, at relatively good interest rates. If you borrow more money than you pay down in debt this year, you will run a deficit. If you pay down more than you borrow, you will run a surplus. The total of all that you owe is your outstanding debt.

Some people have retirement plan investment accounts that allow borrowing up to half the balance, so that you can borrow from yourself and pay the interest owed to yourself. The federal government also borrows from itself. Taxes for Social Security and Medicare are deposited into trust funds that pay those benefits. The Social Security trust fund has been running a surplus for many years; that trust fund has a balance of trillions of dollars held in special federal bonds.[10]

For years the U.S. federal government had the best credit in the world. After World War II ended in 1945, the U.S. was the world's largest economy, the only major industrial power without significant war damage to its homeland, and the world's most technologically advanced nation. While the dollar's value was eroded by inflation over time, the dollar was more stable than many other currencies. The dollar became the world's reserve currency for many years, the currency in which corporations and governments could safely hold their savings and pay their bills. Foreign central banks became major purchasers of U.S. treasury bonds, lowering the interest rates on those bonds.

The History of Federal Debt

"... a public debt is a public curse ..."–James Madison

America's federal government began in an orgy of borrowing and inflation, funding the Revolution with rapidly depreciating paper money and debt that was repeatedly restructured. By 1800, the government's finances were sound and generally in surplus. The government borrowed during major wars (such as the War of 1812 and the Civil War), but otherwise paid down its debt. Federal debt in 1914 was less than 5% of GDP. For World War I, the government borrowed the then huge sum of $24 billion, 75% of its total war spending. Some of that debt was repaid in the 1920s, the last long period of surpluses in U.S. history.[11]

Federal deficits became normal beginning in 1931 when government expanded with new programs in response to the Great Depression that began in 1929. Deficits continued during World War II because of war spending. Since World

War II, deficits have continued and become chronic. In the 77 years from 1931 to 2007, we have had a surplus in 12 years and a deficit in 65 years. The only periods of surplus longer than two years in that time were 1947-1949 and 1998-2001.[12] In both cases, Democratic Presidents (Truman and Clinton) governed with Republican Congresses.[13]

Both Democratic and Republican administrations have run deficits, but recent Republican administrations have been notoriously profligate. From fiscal years 1982 to 1993, when federal budgets were determined by President Reagan (1981-1989) and President George H. W. Bush (1989-1993), the federal government added more than $2.4 trillion in public debt, an average of more than $200 billion per year in new debt. From fiscal years 2002 to 2006, under President George W. Bush, the federal government added more than $1.5 trillion in public debt in five years, an average of more than $300 billion per year in new debt. The federal budget is now in a state of permanent deficit; the Bush administration has forecast a surplus for FY 2012, three years after it leaves office; that forecast is almost certainly wrong, because it does not include likely tax law changes and may be too optimistic about government revenues.[14]

Money Owed to the Public and to the Trust Funds

Both the federal deficit (this year's increase in debt) and the overall federal debt have two versions: the total deficit and debt and the deficit and debt owed outside of the federal government, or "to the public."

In FY 2006, the federal government had a $434 billion general fund deficit minus a $186 billion trust fund surplus for a $248 billion unified deficit, added debt owed to the public. The U.S. Treasury issued $434 billion more in bonds than it paid off, but $186 billion of those bonds are sitting in a filing cabinet (or the computerized equivalent) at the Social Security Administration as part of various trust funds; interest on those bonds is credited to the trust funds.

At the end of FY 2006, the federal government had about $8.5 trillion in outstanding debt, of which $4.8 trillion was debt held by the public and the rest was held by the trust funds and other government accounts. Law imposes a "debt ceiling" which is routinely raised by Congress. The ceiling is about $9 trillion in early 2007.

When we look at immediate federal cash flow and the potential for federal borrowing to crowd out private borrowing and raise interest rates, we look at the unified deficit of $248 billion. The general fund deficit is an ominous preview of future deficits, because the Social Security trust funds will stop running a surplus by about 2017.[15] After 2017, Social Security will add to the unified deficit rather than reducing it.

Consider a family that is a thousand dollars short each month. That family may be paying $600 in interest (after tax savings) on a mortgage, $100 in interest on a car loan, and $200 in interest on credit card balances each month. They realize with regret that if they were not in debt, they would have a much smaller deficit, $100 rather than $1,000 each month. Our federal government is in the same situation. If we did not have this large debt, we would save $227 billion per year in interest; the unified deficit would be $21 billion instead of $248 billion.

Almost all of the money that the federal government uses to pay interest and principal on its debt comes from broad-based taxes on the American people. In a very real sense, you are cosigning the federal government's borrowing. Here is your share and your family's share of new federal debt if we keep borrowing at the current rate:

Cost of New Federal Public Debt (Based on FY 2006 Actual New Debt)

	Cost Each Year	Cost Over a Lifetime
Per Person	$827	$66,160
Per Family	$3,308	$264,640
For Our Country	$248 billion	$19,840 billion

Your share of the $4.8 trillion in debt already held by the public at the end of FY 2006 is about $16,000 per person or $64,000 per family.

Public Debt Relative to GDP and Revenue

Economists commonly evaluate a nation's public debt relative to its GDP. Debt held by the public was about 36% of GDP at the end of FY 2006. However the federal government does not control 100% of economic output; if tax rates rose to 100%, then economic output would drop to near zero. A better measure is the ratio of a government's public debt to its annual revenue. The $4.8 trillion in publicly held debt at the end of FY 2006 was two times the $2.4 trillion in federal revenue that year, a debt to revenue ratio of 200%.

Our Debt to Foreigners

The amount of federal debt held outside the United States is large enough to affect the value of the dollar and potentially our foreign policy. Foreigners own more than $2 trillion in U.S. debt, about 43% of debt held by the public. Foreign official institutions, such as the central banks of other countries (equivalent to our Federal Reserve bank) hold more than $1.3 trillion in federal debt.[16] Interest payments on foreign debt are approaching $100 billion per year, adding to our balance of payments deficit with the rest of the world. China holds more than $400 billion in federal debt,[17] with about $350 billion of that total held by China's central bank.[18] If the U.S. and China are ever in conflict over another issue, such as the status of Taiwan, the Chinese could increase our interest rates and reduce the value of U.S. debt by selling their holdings of U.S. Treasury securities. China is also our largest trading partner and conflict is in neither nation's interest. However nations and their governments have been known to act illogically.

Rolling Over the Debt

Because the debt is large and increasing, our government must constantly issue new debt and use the proceeds to repay old debt, rolling over the debt, similar to the way consumers take out new credit cards and use them to pay down the debt on their older cards.

The majority of the publicly held debt, about $2.5 trillion, is medium-term debt that matures in two to ten years (Treasury Notes). Nearly $1 trillion is short-term debt (Treasury Bills) that matures in one year or less, often within 90 days. Treasury Bonds, maturing in ten to thirty years, and inflation-protected bonds called TIPS, maturing in five to twenty years, total nearly a trillion dollars in additional long-term debt. Non-marketable securities such as savings bonds make up the remaining debt. [19] Because the federal government runs a deficit, has much short-term debt to roll over, and relies on foreign central banks for much of its financing, it is very vulnerable to adverse events, such as a rise in interest rates, a falling value for the dollar causing foreign central banks to hold reserves in other currencies or at least stop accumulating dollar assets, or some international political or military conflict that stops the purchase of U.S. debt by other nations.

Can We Pay Off the Debt?

"I have long argued that paying down the national debt is beneficial for the economy: It keeps interest rates lower than they otherwise would be and frees savings to finance increases in the capital stock, thereby boosting productivity and real incomes."
—Alan Greenspan, then Federal Reserve Chairman, in a speech to the Bond Market Association on April 27, 2001.[20]

It is still conceivable and desirable for the federal government to pay off its public debt. Chapter 11 describes how this book's spending cuts can pay off our public debt.

Federal Debt Trends

Figure 3.1 shows federal debt as a percentage of GDP at ten-year intervals for the last fifty years.

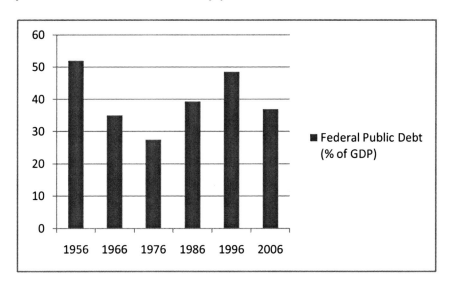

Figure 3.1. Federal Public Debt
1956-2006 (% of GDP)

This data shows *no* consistent historical trend of increasing public debt as a percentage of GDP. The year by year data shows public debt declining from 108.6% of GDP in 1946, at the end of World War II, to 23.9% of GDP in 1974 during the fiscally conservative Nixon administration. Debt then increased to 49.4% of GDP in 1993, largely because of the large deficits in the Reagan and George H. W. Bush administrations. Debt declined to 33.0% of GDP in 2001, in the fiscally conservative Clinton administration. The public debt is increasing again, during the profligate George W. Bush administration, but was still only 37.0% of GDP at the end of FY 2006.[21]

If we discern any mathematical pattern at all in the public debt, it is not a pattern of runaway increase but a pattern of cycles. Debt increases and becomes a greater public concern; fiscally conservative policies are adopted and the debt declines. Later on, with the government's finances in better condition, another administration wins at least temporary power by borrowing for popular purposes, such as wars, entitlements, subsidies, tax cuts, or all of these.

This data does not show a federal budget crisis in the making. There is now a real burden of proof to overcome to demonstrate that a federal budget crisis will happen at all, let alone that such a crisis requires huge spending cuts or tax increases. Providing such real and compelling evidence is the job of the next chapter.

4 THE FEDERAL BUDGET CRISIS

"In the present crisis, government is not the solution to our problem; government is the problem."—President Ronald Reagan in his First Inaugural Address, 1981

A crisis is when things can no longer go on as they have. It is common to postpone a crisis, to evade reality until reality no longer can be evaded. In our personal lives, the postponed crisis has a thousand forms—an employer's dissatisfaction leading to our firing; transferring balances from one credit card to another until we can no longer pay our bills; ignoring a nasty cough after years of smoking, rather than facing the impersonal judgment of the X-ray machine. A crisis does not resolve itself. Postponing a crisis typically makes the consequences more severe.

When a crisis is not direct and personal, we may get our information about it from the media. In early 2007, our media looks like this:

Anna Nicole-Britney-Candidates for President -Global Warming-Housing Bubble-Iran-Iraq-Oil Prices-Stock Markets-Trade Deficits-Walter Reed Army Hospital

Two of 2007's top news stories are the personal problems of a young popular singer and the untimely death of the former stripper who married a billionaire. You cannot judge a problem's importance from the amount of media coverage.

What Makes a Problem Generally Important?

"It's a recession when your neighbor loses his job;
it's a depression when you lose yours."
—Former President Harry S Truman
in Observer, April 13, 1958

What happens in our own lives is important to each of us. Only a few problems in the broader world should be generally important to us all. A generally important problem is wide-ranging, includes us or those we care about, is severe, is probable, and is real, supported by evidence.

Often problems that are not probable or not even real attract attention and significant government funding. For example, our government has spent billions of dollars preparing for a possible major flu epidemic, though the chance of an epidemic in any specific year is small. An example of an unreal problem was in 2002 and 2003, when our government claimed that Iraq was secretly producing weapons of mass destruction (WMDs). With a complete lack of direct evidence, and in the face of major negative evidence from both the Iraqi government and U.N. inspectors, our government invaded and occupied Iraq, at a cost so far of more than $400 billion and more than 3,500 U.S. lives. No significant weapons of mass destruction were ever found.

The Iraq War should teach us another lesson as well. Be very skeptical when a "national emergency" or "crisis" is used to justify more government power or aggression.

The Reliable Evidence for the Federal Budget Crisis

Chapters 2 and 3 showed that the history of federal spending and federal debt for the last fifty years don't show any trend towards a federal budget crisis. The evidence for the federal budget crisis rests on two major claims:

- Federal costs to support retirees, through Social Security and Medicare, will greatly increase as a share of GDP.

- Federal health care spending, for Medicare and Medicaid, will increase as a share of GDP.

Because Medicare is both a retiree program and a health program, its costs increase when either the number of retirees or health care costs increase. Some Medicaid spending is for retiree nursing home care, and that part of Medicaid spending is also affected by both the number of retirees and increasing health care costs.

Evidence for an Increasing Number of Retirees

As shown in Figure 4.1, the two generations born before the Baby Boom have nearly 50 million living members, most already retired. The generation born 7/1/1945 to 6/30/1965 (the Baby Boom and six months before and after), has more than 82 million living members.[22] The oldest Baby Boomers start retiring early on Social Security in 2008; some of the youngest Baby Boomers, who choose to defer Social Security to age 70, will start receiving payments in 2034.

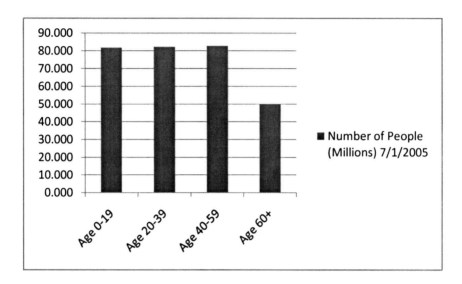

The chart shows a bar graph with the y-axis labeled from 0.000 to 90.000, and x-axis categories: Age 0-19, Age 20-39, Age 40-59, Age 60+. Legend: ■ Number of People (Millions) 7/1/2005

Figure 4.1. U.S. Population by Age (7/1/2005)[23]

Since Social Security began, each generation of retirees was supported by much larger successor generations of workers. Figure 4.1 shows that this is no longer the case. U.S. fertility, the number of children born per woman, fell from about 3.7 children during the Baby Boom to about 2 children since the mid-70s.[24] Each new generation is now about the same size as the previous generation, permanently reducing the number of workers supporting each retiree.

In the first two hundred years of the United States, as our population grew from about three million to over two hundred million, rapid population growth was the norm. Lower birth rates during the Great Depression and World War II increased the relative size of the Baby Boom generation, but it was still normal for it to be much larger than the generations before. The Baby Boom is the beginning of permanent problems for Social Security, not because it is a large generation, but because it is not followed by even larger generations. When the Baby Boomers grew up, they led the U.S. through what is called the *demographic transition*, from high birth rates to much lower birth rates. The demographic transition was encouraged by the universal availability and widespread social acceptance of abortion and contraception, along with social trends that liberated women to choose careers instead of motherhood, to delay marriage, or to not marry at all.

As described in Chapter 8, the average retiree is now living much longer, because of advances in health care, our substantial health spending, and better health habits.

Table 4.1 shows the projected effects of the demographic transition and longer life spans. The share of U.S. population over 65 (most receiving Social Security, Medicare, or equivalent government pension benefits) grows from less than 13% of population in 2010 to more than 20% by 2050.

Table 4.1. Projected Shares of Population 20 to 64, 65 and Over[25]

Year	% Age 20-64	% Age 65+	Ratio
2010	60.0	12.9	4.65
2015	59.1	14.4	4.10
2020	57.4	16.3	3.52
2025	55.4	18.2	3.04
(jump forward 25 years; no projections given for intermediate years)			
2050	53.5	20.7	2.58

As the share of population 65 and over grows, the share that is ages 20 to 64, the prime ages for working, shrinks. As a result, the ratio of working-age population to retirement-age population drops from 4.65 in 2010 to 2.58 by 2050, an 80% increase in the relative burden that retirees place on workers.

Some in the working-age population don't work outside the home. Chapter 8 gives projections for the actual number of covered workers per Social Security beneficiary, numbers that show the same trend just described.

These kinds of numbers, involving population and how long people live, are some of the most reliable statistics available. There are entire professions, demographers and actuaries, devoted to population calculations and the related financial calculations. The consensus of these experts is that Social Security costs and related Medicare and Medicaid costs will increase greatly in coming years as a major cause of a federal budget crisis.

Evidence for Increasing Federal Per-Person Health Costs

The increasing number of retirees will increase the number of people receiving Medicare or having nursing home care paid by Medicaid. There is also strong evidence that real spending per beneficiary will increase:

- Medicare's Board of Trustees estimates that real spending per beneficiary will increase by 2.5% each year for the next several decades.[26] These projections are the basis for some of the "federal budget crisis" claims, but may be conservative and the problem may be worse.

- The historical growth rate of real health spending per person (all spending, not just federally funded) was over

4% per year from 1945 to 1990 and 3.7% from 1990 to 2002, or much higher than Medicare's projections.[27]

- Medicare's real per beneficiary cost, in 2006 dollars, rose from $1,793 in 1970 to $8,285 in 2005, a 362% increase in 35 years or an annual real growth rate of 4.47%.[28]

- Both Medicare and Medicaid are designed to encourage overspending, with small out-of-pocket costs for health care consumers. Medicaid matches each dollar that states spend with an added dollar or more from the federal government, creating another incentive for overspending.

- The share of population over 85 is growing faster than the share over 65. Those over 85 will be 2% of population in 2010 and 4.9% of population in 2050.[29] Those over 85 have much higher average health care costs than those ages 65 to 84, and are much more likely to receive Medicaid-paid nursing home care, which can cost more than $70,000 per year per person.

- Politicians, drug companies, health care providers, health care workers, and groups representing the elderly and disabled may all support expanding federal health care entitlements and spending. For example, a major new Medicare drug benefit, Part D, was added in 2005, without any major new revenue to pay for that benefit.

For all these reasons it is completely plausible that federal per beneficiary health care spending will grow faster than inflation and faster than economic growth, unless we adopt major reforms, some of which are suggested in this book.

Secondary Causes of the Crisis

The primary causes of the impending federal budget crisis are commitments to retirees and for health care. There are four secondary causes:

Debt   As described in Chapter 3, we added $248 billion to the federal debt in FY 2006 and paid out $227 billion in interest on $4.8 trillion in debt held by the public. Federal deficits and debt are now normal and have huge costs.

Spending   Our government has thousands of giveaway programs that subsidize hundreds of special interests. Chapters 6, 9, and 10 describe how we can cut unneeded spending.

War   We spent $522 billion on our military in FY 2006, including two ongoing wars. Chapter 7 describes how to cut our military spending.

Tax cuts   The George W. Bush administration cut taxes multiple times while increasing every category of government spending. Tax cuts may be desirable, especially for taxpayers, but are disastrous if the government increases spending and relies on borrowing instead.

We could manage for many years with one or two of these fiscal problems. The combination of all these problems means that federal finances are in serious trouble.

Putting It All Together: the GAO Projections

The Government Accountability Office (GAO) monitors federal government spending and programs. Under Comptroller General of the United States David M. Walker, the agency has been sounding the alarm about the federal budget crisis. GAO projects the future federal budget using two sets of assumptions. An "alternative" projection, called *current* in this book, extends current policies into the future, making the Bush tax cuts permanent and continuing significant spending on other government programs. The *baseline* projection assumes that the Bush tax cuts expire, taxes increase, and that we significantly reduce the share of GDP going to other government programs. The baseline projection combines increased taxes and major, unspecified spending cuts, perhaps some of the cuts in this book.

Because the current projection reflects current government policy, this book focuses on the current projection, summarized in Table 4.2. These projections show Social Security's relative burden increasing by about 60% by 2031, and Medicare and Medicaid's relative burden increasing by 133% by 2031. Ten years before that, by 2021, federal deficits will have reached an unsustainable level of more than 6% of GDP, an annual deficit of more than one trillion dollars.

Table 4.2. GAO Current Projection % of GDP
(Tax Cuts Continued, Other Spending Stays High)[30]

Year	SS	MC/ MA	OTH.	INT.	TOT.	REV.	+/-	DEBT
2006	4.2	3.9	10.5	1.7	20.3	18.4	- 1.9	37.0
2011	4.3	4.7	9.8	1.8	20.5	17.7	- 2.9	39.3
2016	4.7	5.5	9.6	2.3	22.1	17.7	- 4.4	49.7
2021	5.4	6.7	9.5	3.1	24.7	18.4	- 6.2	66.9
2026	6.2	7.8	9.5	4.3	27.9	18.5	- 9.4	95.1
2031	6.7	9.1	9.5	6.2	31.5	18.6	- 12.9	136.5

SS=Social Security, MC/MA=Medicare and Medicaid, OTH=Other
INT.=Net Interest, TOT.=Total Spending, REV.=Revenue, +/-=Deficit

Table 4.3 shows the baseline projection, which delays the federal budget crisis by about 15 years, to 2036, through a combination of significant tax increases and significant spending cuts.

Table 4.3. GAO Baseline Projection % of GDP
(Tax Cuts Expire, Other Spending Restrained)[31]

Year	SS	MC/ MA	OTH.	INT.	TOT.	REV.	+/-	DEBT
2006	4.2	3.9	10.5	1.7	20.3	18.4	- 1.9	37.0
2011	4.3	4.5	8.9	1.6	19.3	19.2	-0.1	32.8
2016	4.7	5.3	7.9	1.2	19.1	20.0	0.9	22.1
2021	5.4	6.4	7.8	0.8	20.3	20.1	-0.1	15.9
2026	6.0	7.5	7.8	0.9	22.2	20.1	-2.0	19.4
2031	6.5	8.6	7.8	1.4	24.2	20.1	-4.1	31.9
2036	6.7	9.6	7.8	2.3	26.4	20.1	-6.3	52.7
2041	6.8	10.5	7.8	3.7	28.7	20.1	-8.5	81.4
2046	6.8	11.3	7.8	5.4	31.2	20.1	-11.0	117.9

SS=Social Security, MC/MA=Medicare and Medicaid, OTH=Other
INT.=Net Interest, TOT.=Total Spending, REV.=Revenue, +/-=Deficit

How Important a Problem Is the Federal Budget Crisis?

"... the U.S. government's major reported liabilities, social insurance commitments and other fiscal exposures continue to grow. They now total approximately $50 trillion—about four times the nation's total output (GDP) in fiscal year 2006."—David M. Walker, Comptroller General of the United States, January 23, 2007[32]

Our federal finances are out of balance and will produce a major federal budget crisis in coming decades. The range of this problem is 300 million U.S. residents and another 100 million who will be born or immigrate in coming decades. It affects our entire nation directly and indirectly affects other nations that are allies or trading partners. The problem is severe, with costs in the tens of trillions of dollars for the nation and in the hundreds of thousands of dollars per U.S. family. Major cuts in government spending or major tax increases will directly affect tens of millions of Americans.

Unlike the risk of a flu pandemic or a terrorist attack, the federal budget crisis is a certain and definite problem. It will produce bad results in the next 10 to 30 years unless we take major action to solve the problem.

Unlike the flimsy, indirect, and false evidence given for Iraqi WMD programs in 2002-2003, the evidence for the federal budget crisis is detailed, direct, and authoritative. This evidence comes directly from federal budget documents, federal financial reports, and federal agency publications. All of these documents are freely available on the Internet.

When Will the Sky Fall?

"The sky is falling!"—Chicken Little

We can identify certain lines that it would be bad for the federal budget to cross, based on our history and the experiences of other nations. For example, advanced countries do not normally have debt greater than 110% of GDP.[33] The second line that is bad to cross based on U.S. budget history is a unified deficit, net new public debt in a year, of more than 5% of GDP, a level reached only twice since 1946 and not at all since 1985.[34] Table 4.4 shows in what years we will cross these red lines using the GAO's current and baseline assumptions.

Table 4.4. When Will the Sky Fall?

Event	Year for Current Assumptions	Year for Baseline Assumptions
Deficit More Than 5% of GDP	2019	2033
Public Debt More Than 110% of GDP	2028	2045

In both of the GAO projections, deficit, debt, and total federal spending go into an impossible upwards spiral in subsequent years, impossible because creditors won't loan us the money to keep rolling over the debt when federal finances are in such bad shape.

Financial projections for Social Security[35] and Medicare[36] also give us certain dates:

2004 Medicare HI (Hospitalization Insurance) trust fund spends more than its tax revenue (has already happened, there was a slight surplus in 2005 and a return to deficits in 2006).

2017 Social Security spends more than its tax revenue, a key date because Social Security will begin adding to the general fund deficit instead of reducing it.

2019 Medicare HI trust fund exhausted; HI tax revenues will pay an estimated 80% of expenses.

2041 Social Security trust fund exhausted; an estimated 25% cut in all benefit checks unless Congress appropriates general fund revenue.

So we expect the federal budget to be more and more out of balance by 2019 with the problems rapidly getting worse unless we reform the budget and the budget process.

Figure 4.2 shows how federal deficits will get much worse in future years without major changes.

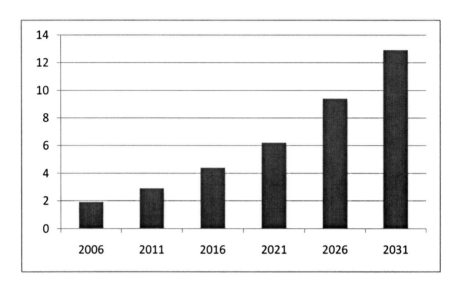

Figure 4.2. Future Federal Deficits (% of GDP)[37]

On our current course, federal finances will go out of control as soon as 2019, a dozen years away. Chapter 5 describes what federal bankruptcy could do to our country.

5 FEDERAL BANKRUPTCY

"… if the United States doesn't come to our senses and get our act together, we could eventually suffer the same fate as Argentina. That nation defaulted on its debt, which had a significant adverse effect on the country's economy and the living standards of most of its citizens."—David M. Walker, Comptroller General of the United States[38]

You will never see the U.S. President, hat in hand, walk into a courtroom to declare our country bankrupt and seek the protection of U.S. Code Title 11, the Bankruptcy Code.

It seems unlikely that a superpower, the great victor of World War II, spanning a continent, governing hundreds of millions of diverse people, with an economic and political system emulated by dozens of allied nations, could go bankrupt. This nation reliably paid its debts for decades, so the tripling of foreign debt in a six-year period is not a cause for concern.[39] The foreign war weakening its military and finances is small in proportion to the nation's resources. It *seems* unlikely, but the Soviet Union did go bankrupt and also dissolved as a nation and an empire, consigned to the dustbin of history since 1991.

Nations have been going broke for centuries. In the hundred years from 1571 to 1670, Spain went bankrupt seven times; in the thirty years from 1633 to 1662, France went bankrupt three times. During the Napoleonic wars, half of Europe went bankrupt in the five years from 1809 to 1813, including Spain, the Netherlands, Sweden, Russia, and Denmark.[40]

Bankruptcy by Default

Countries, like individuals, sometimes just stop paying the bills they owe, *defaulting* on their debts. Argentina defaulted on its international debt of $93 billion in 2002. That nation was unable to borrow money for four years after defaulting. Most bond holders surrendered their bonds for one third of the original value.[41] The peso's value dropped by 75%, the economy crashed, and unemployment exceeded 25%.[42]

Bankruptcy by Hyperinflation

Without officially defaulting, a government can eliminate its debt burden through *hyperinflation*, printing so much paper money that the currency becomes worthless. Hyperinflation destroys both the debt burden and every asset held in a nation's currency, wiping out the value of savings accounts, bonds, pensions, and other financial instruments. Hyperinflation is not rare; it has happened in five of the world's 25 largest economies during the past 20 years: Argentina, Brazil, Poland, Russia, and Turkey.[43] Note that Argentina has used both hyperinflation and outright default at different times to wipe out its debts. A hyperinflation often ends with the introduction of a new currency to replace a now worthless old currency. For example, each new 1992 Argentina peso was exchanged for 100,000,000,000 (one hundred billion) of the debased pre-1983 pesos.

Argentina is a good example of what the United States could go through. Both countries have large land areas and ample natural resources relative to their populations. Both are multi-ethnic countries inhabited by immigrants and the descendants of immigrants from all over the world. Argentina's economy has been wrecked by nearly a century of statist policies, emphasizing government control, taxation, default, and debasement of the currency. In 1913, Argentina's standard of living was the same as in Europe.[44] Today, its standard of living is half that of Europe[45], even though Argentina was not held back by the two world wars and the Cold War that took place in Europe since 1913.

More moderate inflation, such as devaluing the dollar by 15% per year, is not helpful for our government in dealing with its debt for two reasons. First, Social Security pensions and government pensions are adjusted annually for inflation. Second, interest rates would increase because those lending money want some real rate of return. If inflation were 15% per year, then interest rates could exceed 20%. If the federal government had to pay 20% interest on five trillion dollars or more in debt held by the public, then federal net interest payments would eventually increase four-fold to more than a trillion dollars a year.

Harsh Spending Cuts

When a bankrupt government can no longer issue new debt, because no one will buy it, it can no longer sustain past levels of spending. The resulting spending cuts can be harsh:

- Russia's state pensions (the equivalent of our Social Security) were cut to below subsistence levels[46] and now are typically $60 per month, often only one tenth of a worker's pre-retirement salary.[47]

- In the 1990's Russian military pay dropped to below subsistence levels. Soldiers, including the officers and enlisted men responsible for Russia's nuclear missiles, were not paid for many months.[48]

As the main successor state to the bankrupt Soviet Union, Russia was bankrupt for much of the 1990s. Today Russia runs a budget surplus and is in a better financial condition than the United States.

In the U.S. federal budget, Congress can cut discretionary spending at any time; such spending stops if Congress does not agree on appropriations or a "continuing" authorization for the next year's spending. Mandatory spending, mostly on entitlements such as Social Security and welfare, continues automatically without new legislation, but Congress can cut this spending by agreeing on changes to the authorizing laws.

Social Security is not exempt from spending cuts. The Supreme Court has repeatedly held that there is no property right in Social Security benefits.[49] The Social Security law allows and requires major benefit cuts when the Social Security trust fund is exhausted. The Social Security trustees predict that the trust fund will be exhausted in 2041 and that benefit checks will then be immediately cut by 25%.[50]

Harsh Tax Increases

"Here are some options: a 70 percent increase in personal and corporate income taxes [or] a 109 percent hike in payroll taxes"[51]*–Laurence J. Kotlikoff, prominent economist and coauthor of* The Coming Generational Storm

How will a family earning $100,000 per year react if their federal income tax bracket goes from 25% to 42%? Would it be any better to raise their payroll tax rate (shared by employees and employers) from 15.3% to 32% of salary?

It would take tax increases of this size, adopted immediately, to avoid federal bankruptcy solely through tax increases. Such tax increases could also lead to economic collapse and massive tax evasion, not achieving their desired goals.

A major increase in tax revenue without major harm to the economy would require radical tax reform that broadens the tax base, eliminating many credits, deductions, exemptions, and *tax expenditures*, subsidies delivered via tax provisions.

Economists have designed improved tax systems, but tax systems are adopted by politicians, not economists. Our elected officials would offend banks, builders, charities, churches, educators, health insurance companies, homeowners, and tax professionals if they eliminated the current Internal Revenue Code.

While this book describes how to solve our fiscal problems entirely with spending cuts, it is worthwhile to understand what part of those problems could be solved with tax increases that are similar to past federal taxes, taxes that did not ruin our economy. Since 1946, federal revenues have ranged from 14.4% to 20.9% of GDP, with almost all years in the 17-20% range.[52] Tax increases from 18.4% of GDP in FY 2006 to 20.0% of GDP, the tax level in the boom years of 1998 and 1999, would increase revenue by $209 billion[53], still leaving 80% of our fiscal gap to close with spending cuts.

Gridlock and Government Shutdowns

We will not resolve a trillion dollar federal budget crisis without disagreement and discord. Those who are net taxpayers and receive few government services will strongly oppose much higher taxes and be willing to cut spending. Those who rely on government funding, including government employees and the elderly, will tend to favor higher taxes while maintaining spending. Any one voter may belong to groups with contradictory interests, such as an older worker with both Social Security and wage income, wanting an unreduced Social Security check and also not wanting higher taxes on wages.

Almost all fiscal policy must come from Congress, through appropriations, authorizations, and tax laws. When a legislature fails to agree on needed legislation, large parts of a government can actually shut down, which happened twice in 1995 for our federal government, and has happened in 2005 to 2006 in Minnesota, New Jersey, and Puerto Rico.[54]

On our present course, the federal budget crisis will arrive by 2019, unless world events bring it on sooner.

How Federal Bankruptcy Could Happen Much Sooner

History does not move in straight lines or gentle curves. Thousands of pages of budgets and government reports assume steady, moderate economic growth for the indefinite future. Consider that a book about federal finances written in 1907 and forecasting the future of the federal budget would not have forecast the First World War, nor the Depression, nor ending the gold standard and inflating the dollar.

We know that shocks happen in our history. The weakened state of our federal finances makes the United States much more vulnerable to these shocks:

Oil prices The world will not run out of oil. However possible peak production of low-cost oil and increasing oil demand from China, India, and other countries could lead to much higher prices.

Recession The U.S. currently has large federal deficits when the economy has been expanding for years. Any major economic contraction, a recession or depression, will increase the deficit.

Terror A major terrorist attack on the U.S. homeland, like 9/11 or larger, especially with weapons of mass destruction, could reduce economic output and federal revenues while increasing federal costs. (Such an attack creates obvious humanitarian concerns; the focus in this discussion is the impact on federal finances.)

Trade The U.S. trade deficit hit a record $763.6 billion dollars in 2006. [55] We are exporting paper money and various financial instruments, such as U.S. Treasury debt, in exchange for imports of tangible goods like cars, electronics, and oil. If the world's appetite for dollars diminishes, then the dollar's value falls, the prices of imported goods rise, and U.S. interest rates will rise.

War   If the United States is involved in new foreign wars, those conflicts could add hundreds of billions to trillions of dollars in costs. In the past hundred years the U.S. has been involved in two huge world wars, and five major smaller wars (Korea, Vietnam, Persian Gulf, Afghanistan, and Iraq), averaging a new war every 14 years.

Understanding Nearly Fifty Trillion Dollars in Federal Liabilities

The *2006 Financial Report of the United States Government* lists federal liabilities of $49.3 trillion, shown in Table 5.1.[56]

Table 5.1. Federal Liabilities

Liability	Billions
Present value of future Medicare deficits	$32,305
Present value of future Social Security deficits	$6,449
Federal debt held by the public	$4,868
Federal employee and veterans benefits	$4,679
Miscellaneous liabilities	$866
Present value of future Railroad Ret. deficits	$101
Total Federal Liabilities	**$49,268**

Liabilities for Medicare are two thirds of the total; liabilities for Social Security plus Medicare are almost four fifths of the total. The federal government does not list future Medicaid spending as a liability though it projects that Medicaid will contribute significantly to future deficits.

The trend in federal liabilities is very bad, as pointed out in Chapter 1, increasing from about $20 trillion in 2000 to about $50 trillion in 2006.[57]

The Trillion Dollar Fiscal Gap

Per the GAO's projections of current federal government policies, our fiscal gap is 7.4% of GDP.[58] If we permanently cut federal government spending or increase federal government revenues by that share of our economic output, we will keep our government's debt and liabilities from growing out of control.

In FY 2006, 7.4% of GDP was $966 billion. Because the costs of balancing our federal finances are greater the longer we wait, this book's goal is to find $1,000 billion or $1 trillion in spending cuts when analyzing the FY 2006 federal budget.

Dr. Kent Smetters and Dr. Jagadeesh Gokhale, who conducted the first systematic studies of the federal fiscal gap, coined the apt term *menu of pain* to describe the choices of massive tax increases or massive spending cuts to close the federal fiscal gap.[59] Dealing with this kind of menu requires a complete change in our politicians.

The Government That Says No

"It is incumbent on every generation to pay its own debts as it goes."—Thomas Jefferson

The most dangerous promise is one that someone else must keep. For several decades, office-holders elected for two, four, or six years have gained and kept office by making promises that won't come due for decades: the government will take care of you in retirement; the government will pay all your medical bills after age 65; the government will repay a 30-year bond to cover today's desired spending. For several decades office-holders have said yes to every group seeking federal funding, until now federal obligations are out of control and those long delayed bills are coming due.

For this generation to begin to live up to Jefferson's words, we must make a 180 degree turn, from a government that says yes to everything and everyone to a government that says no to whatever it cannot reasonably afford. The next five chapters show us how to do that.

6 STOP THE GIVEAWAYS

"Everyone wants to live at the expense of the State. They forget that the State lives at the expense of everyone."—Frederic Bastiat

We tolerate taxes and government spending for broad public purposes: to provide for the common defense, promote the general welfare, and secure the blessings of liberty. When government instead picks our pockets to support particular politically favored special interests, it wastes our money and loses legitimacy.

This chapter suggests that we stop giving away federal money in seven ways: for earmarked "pork," farmers, encouraging debt, foreign aid, long-term disaster relief and insurance, corporate welfare, and medical education.

Make Congress Kosher: End the Pork

"It could probably be shown by facts and figures that there is no distinctly native American criminal class except Congress."—Mark Twain

Five centuries ago Europe's dominant institution fell into moral disgrace and was permanently divided. That institution was the Catholic church. Church officials were aggressively selling "indulgences," documents promising forgiveness of sins, to raise money for the church and for themselves. Those who ran the temple had become the money changers in the temple. The reformist monk Martin

Luther nailed his 95 Theses to a church door in Wittenberg, beginning the Protestant Reformation.

Today the revenues of a great nation are being sold by members of Congress, for pennies on the dollar from lobbyists or contributors, or sometimes for simple vanity. This is the spending called *pork*, money typically requested by individual members of Congress and not by the President's budget or via a Congressional hearing. Pork is money for a specific local project or special interest, money not requested by the agency that must spend it.

Citizens Against Government Waste (CAGW) has tracked Congress's spending on pork for years. These examples are from its *2006 Congressional Pig Book*, which lists 9,963 pork projects costing a total of $29 billion:

- $500,000 for a teapot museum in North Carolina

- More than $13 million to an Irish group for the World Toilet Summit

- Nearly $600 million for aircraft that the Defense Department doesn't want and rates unsatisfactory

These pork items and thousands of others are put into the federal budget via *earmarks*, designations for specific projects added to the budget by members of Congress. In fiscal year 2005 there were more than 15,000 earmarks totaling nearly $37 billion.[60] This book assumes savings only for projects that CAGW has identified as wasteful pork, 29 billion dollars per year in 2006, reduced to 24 billion dollars because some programs are cut elsewhere in this book.

Pork has exploded in recent years. For example, President Reagan vetoed a transportation bill in 1987 because it contained 121 earmarked projects. The 2005 Congress put 6,300 earmarks into that year's transportation bill.[61]

Pork doesn't just add to existing spending, sometimes it diverts spending. Government spending on science and academic research is increasingly earmarked rather than determined by any sort of peer review or merit. For example, Senator Harry Reid (D-Nevada) diverted a fifth of the National Renewable Energy Laboratory's budget to projects in his home state, causing major budget cuts and layoffs at NREL in Golden, Colorado.[62] Earmarking of research funds is so bad that one great American university, the Massachusetts Institute of Technology, refuses to accept any earmarked funds.[63]

Here are some notorious examples of pork and earmarks:[64]

- Rep. Allan Mollohan (D-West Virginia) directed $250 million to five organizations that he set up, organizations run by his friends and former employees.

- $37 million in defense money was given to a private company that bribed Rep. Randy "Duke" Cunningham (R-California), now in federal prison.

- Senator Lisa Murkowski (R-Alaska) tried to earmark $223 million for the infamous "Bridge to Nowhere," which would have connected Ketchikan, Alaska to an island where only 50 people live. The Senator's family owns property on the island.

There are principled members of Congress who abstain from pork spending. Representative Jeff Flake (R-Arizona), interviewed by 60 Minutes in November 2006, has consistently and continuously opposed earmarks and pork.

In early 2007 there was much talk of earmark reform. Initial FY 2007 earmark totals were lower because just two of eleven appropriations bills were finished before the fiscal year began.

To end or greatly reduce earmarks and pork will require authorizing the President to withhold funds from unworthy projects (impoundment), making earmarks more public, and limiting how Congress can add earmarks. These steps are described in more detail in Chapter 12.

End Pork Savings[65]

	Saved Each Year	Saved in a Lifetime
Per Person	$80	$6,400
Per Family	$320	$25,600
For Our Country	$24 billion	$1,920 billion
Only 83% of pork is counted as savings because of the overlap with other cuts recommended in this book.[66]		

End Farm Programs

"Agriculture, manufactures, commerce and navigation, the four pillars of our prosperity, are most thriving when left most free to individual enterprise."—Thomas Jefferson in his First Annual Message as President[67]

A free economy contains ten thousand different trades and professions: the nurse exchanging her work for the shop owner's; the computer programmer exchanging his work for the auto mechanic's; the preacher exchanging his work for the farmer's. Of all these occupations, only one has an entire cabinet department of the federal government devoted to subsidizing, informing, and regulating it: the U.S. Department of Agriculture.

Most farm subsidies are for a few major crops and commodities, notably corn, cotton, and dairy products. Most farms, farmers, and farm products receive no subsidies at all. Three fifths of U.S. farm output is not subsidized. Subsidies are geographically concentrated as well. More than half of subsidies go to 25 of America's 435 Congressional districts.[68]

Most farm subsidies go to 1,300 large corporations and large farmers, who are much wealthier than the average American family. Farm programs are Robin Hood in reverse, taking from the poor and giving to the relatively rich. More than a billion dollars has been paid to wealthy landowners who don't farm at all; they own land last farmed more than twenty years ago; the government promised open-ended payments tied to the land.[69]

Farm commodity price supports double or triple some food prices, hurting all American consumers and hurting poor households the most. For example, because of federal sugar subsidies and other controls, sugar prices in the U.S. are almost three times the world price.[70] Higher food prices caused by federal farm programs (both subsidies and import restrictions) cost American families more than $16 billion annually in higher food prices, in addition to the tax monies spent on subsidies.[71]

U.S. farm subsidies hurt farmers in the developing world. Cotton farmers in sub-Saharan Africa, one of the world's poorest regions, are starving because subsidized U.S. cotton is dumped on the world market.[72] Farm subsidies by Europe and the U.S. were a major reason that world trade talks collapsed in 2006, preventing improvements in trade.[73]

Farm subsidies encourage environmentally destructive policies, including growing crops in places that make no sense in a free market. For example, we subsidize growing cotton, which needs lots of water, in the Arizona desert.[74]

Farm programs were established in 1933. The United States survived for 157 years before these programs were established. We can learn from New Zealand's experience. New Zealand eliminated all farm subsidies in 1987 without major problems.[75]

End Farm Programs Savings[76]

	Saved Each Year	Saved in a Lifetime
Per Person	$116	$9,280
Per Family	$464	$37,120
For Our Country	$34.8 billion	$2,784 billion
Eliminates all Department of Agriculture spending other than the Forest Service and the Food and Nutrition Service (food stamps). Credit activity for agriculture is cut in the next section, "Stop Subsidizing Debt."		

Stop Subsidizing Debt

"Neither a borrower nor a lender be."
—Polonius in Hamlet by William Shakespeare

Most adult Americans know from personal experience that debt is bad. If we are lucky enough to have a regular paycheck, we see it disappear to make the mortgage payment, the car payment, and credit card payments.

On the other hand, when Sam, the richest fellow in town, knocked on your door and offered you a big loan, low interest, and years to repay, you were tempted—tempted to buy a boat, start a business, or expand a farm. Sam knocked on a lot of doors and soon the town was booming, a temporary boom fueled by borrowed money. You heard that for every dollar Sam loaned directly, he cosigned loans for another five dollars down at the bank. Even though Sam lived in the biggest house in town, the big white house with the spacious lawn and the rose garden, you started to hear rumors that he was deep in debt himself, that he was spending more than he earned and spreading his own IOUs all over town. As you struggled with your own debts, you wondered whether Sam's encouragement to take on more debt really helped you in the long run. You resolved not to loan money or cosign loans yourself.

Our federal government has more than one hundred loan or loan guarantee programs. It loans money directly, often at subsidized low interest rates, or guarantees (like cosigning) that loans will be repaid, repaying loans when borrowers default. At the end of FY 2006 there was $251 billion in outstanding federal direct loans and more than $1.3 trillion dollars in outstanding federally guaranteed loans.[77]

Federal provision of debt and credit is not due to any shortage of credit in the private sector. Both consumers and businesses are inundated with loan offers. When a person or business cannot borrow easily, it is usually for good reasons, such as past failures to pay bills or a lack of income to repay debt.

Federal loans or guarantees go to farmers, fishermen, real estate developers, exporters, and other businesses, especially those with political connections. For example, the 2005 energy bill contained special language to provide huge federal loan guarantees for a new company started by four former Enron executives.[78]

Beginning in the 1930's, one kind of government loan guarantee was used by millions of Americans, home mortgage guarantees from the Federal Housing Administration and later the Veterans Administration. The FHA and VA still guarantee some mortgages, but these agencies are no longer major players in the home mortgage market. Recent FHA and VA mortgages have often been "sub-prime" mortgages with low or no down payments, the sort of mortgage that is now going into foreclosure, costly to the government, the banks, and the homeowners.[79] In an eight trillion dollar U.S. mortgage market, the several billion dollars of FHA and VA mortgages won't be missed.

One government loan program that will be especially missed by America's middle class is student loans for college costs. However the main effect of these loans has been to increase college tuitions and other costs by as much money as the loans have provided.[80] Students get the same amount of education and now leave college deep in debt.

Establishing the principle that the federal government does not loan money, subsidize loans, or guarantee loans will simplify government, save taxpayers significant sums, and reduce government distortion of financial markets.

Stop Subsidizing Debt Savings[81]

	Saved Each Year	Saved in a Lifetime
Per Person	$80	$6,400
Per Family	$320	$25,600
For Our Country	$24 billion	$1,920 billion

End Foreign Aid

After World War II, the United States began giving money away as part of our international Cold War competition with the communist countries, a competition that ended in 1991. While some foreign aid helps poor people in developing nations, most aid supports U.S. foreign policy goals or business interests. When the U.S. and other developed nations provide aid for development or humanitarian assistance, that aid is often not effective.

The $22 billion of annual U.S. foreign aid includes:

- More than two billion dollars for Israel, one of the world's wealthier nations, mostly in "Foreign Military Financing" for the Israeli military.[82] Israel has its own advanced arms industry that sells hundreds of million dollars in weapons each year. If other nations buy weapons from us, they can do so without taxpayer subsidies.

- Significant funding of the Palestinian National Authority, which many Americans consider a terrorist organization. In FY 2003, the United States provided more than $200 million to the Palestinian government. Most of that money went straight into the pockets of Yasser Arafat and his cronies.[83] Arafat has since died and the Hamas terrorist group[84] now controls much of the Palestinian territory. The U.S. has aided both sides in the Middle East conflict for decades, a system institutionalized after the Camp David accords in 1978.

- More than one billion dollars for anti-narcotics programs, funding the destruction of crops in Afghanistan, Bolivia, Colombia, and other countries that grow opium or coca. These programs make the United States an enemy of the farmers, undermine any good will we might otherwise have in these nations, and do not prevent vast quantities of drugs from being available in the United States, which is where we should deal with U.S. drug problems.[85]

- More than one billion dollars for information and exchange programs, including an $80 million "National Endowment for Democracy" that is designed specifically to meddle in the internal politics of other nations, not a good way to make friends abroad.

Many authors, most recently William Easterly[86], have pointed out that hundreds of billions of dollars in aid to Africa and other very poor countries have produced no results, while China did not rely on aid but simply adopted free market economic policies, producing an economic boom for the last 25 years that has increased per person income by more than 300%.[87]

The U.S. nonprofit sector provides much better ways to help people in other countries. One U.S.-based charity, Christian Children's Fund, spends $180 million per year helping more than ten million children in the developing world.[88] There are dozens of organizations like CCF, many of them efficient and reputable. Internet tools like Charity Navigator[89] help donors ensure that their money is used wisely.

End Foreign Aid Savings[90]

	Saved Each Year	Saved in a Lifetime
Per Person	$74	$5,920
Per Family	$296	$23,680
For Our Country	$22.3 billion	$1,784 billion

End Long-Term Disaster Relief and Insurance

It should not be the federal government's job to stand between people and the consequences of their own action or inaction. If people move to or remain in cities built below sea level or built on major fault lines, then there are ways that people can protect themselves without government, through private insurance and reasonable preparations.

If New Orleans sinks beneath a hurricane's waves, then of course our National Guard and other military resources should assist with immediate aid, followed by an outpouring of voluntary national charity. What is a great and grave mistake is to conscript the tax resources of the entire nation to rebuild New Orleans or any other city. When Chicago was destroyed by fire in 1871, Galveston by hurricane in 1900, and San Francisco by earthquake in 1906, those cities all rebuilt without tens of billions of federal dollars.

The rebuilding at federal expense of New Orleans after Hurricanes Katrina and Rita in 2005 and of parts of New York after 9/11/2001 is a bad and mistaken precedent. If a major earthquake hits Los Angeles or a future hurricane levels Miami, we should not send the bill to Colorado, Tennessee, and the other states.

Not providing long-term aid after disasters may seem callous and hard-hearted, but such expenses are huge and ruinous to the budget. Federal spending on Hurricanes Katrina and Rita alone may total more than $110 billion, spread over multiple years.[91] Payments from federally provided flood insurance for those two hurricanes are expected to total $21 billion. The government has been writing many more flood insurance policies in the Gulf states since those hurricanes and is now at risk for over $1 trillion in coverage nationwide.[92] While writing this book, paid advertising from the federal flood insurance program popped up on my computer, spending taxpayer money to encourage me to seek flood insurance and the accompanying subsidies.

We should no longer use federal money to fund long-term disaster recovery; eliminate the Federal Emergency Management Agency (FEMA), which was generally ineffective after the hurricanes; no longer compensate victims of disaster or terrorism as was done after the 9/11 attacks; and stop providing federal flood insurance, terrorism risk insurance, and airline war risk insurance.

End Long-Term Disaster Relief and Insurance Savings[93]

	Saved Each Year	Saved in a Lifetime
Per Person	$74	$5,920
Per Family	$296	$23,680
For Our Country	$22.3 billion	$1,784 billion
Disaster spending varies greatly from year to year. This estimate is based on FEMA spending for FY 2006, not including spending in other agencies.		

End Corporate Welfare

"Government 'help' to business is just as disastrous as government persecution... the only way a government can be of service to national prosperity is by keeping its hands off."—Ayn Rand[94]

Have you ever heard of the Partnership for a New Generation of Vehicles? Probably not, because the partnership never produced that next generation vehicle. The federal government gave more than $1.5 billion in subsidies to U.S. auto manufacturers over eight years to develop hybrid cars. Hundreds of thousands of American families are driving fuel efficient hybrid cars, but those cars were produced by the unsubsidized Japanese companies Toyota and Honda.[95]

Subsidies to businesses shift resources around and often destroy wealth, but rarely create any long-term prosperity. Chris Edwards of the Cato Institute estimated federal "corporate welfare" spending at $90 billion in 2002.[96] However much of that corporate welfare is in other categories where this book recommends cuts, such as farm subsidies and credit programs. The following savings are based on eliminating the Small Business Administration (SBA), several programs in the Department of Commerce, and some programs in the Department of Energy.

End Corporate Welfare Savings[97]

	Saved Each Year	Saved in a Lifetime
Per Person	$30	$2,400
Per Family	$120	$9,600
For Our Country	$9 billion	$720 billion

Stop Subsidizing Medical Education

Buried deep in the federal budgets for Health and Human Services and Medicare are billions of dollars in subsidies for medical education, mostly to educate doctors or subsidize large teaching hospitals. Doctors and other medical professionals are paid much better than the average American. We have no shortage of doctors; from 1960 to 2000 the number of doctors per 100,000 Americans doubled.[98] The people and institutions in medicine can pay for their own educational programs without subsidies.

Stop Subsidizing Medical Education Savings[99]

	Saved Each Year	Saved in a Lifetime
Per Person	$31	$2,480
Per Family	$124	$9,920
For Our Country	$9.4 billion	$752 billion

The seven proposals in this chapter will immediately save the federal budget $145.8 billion each year, more than 14% of our one trillion dollar target.

7 DECLARE PEACE

"Every gun that is made, every warship launched, every rocket fired signifies, in the final sense, a theft from those who hunger and are not fed, those who are cold and are not clothed.

This world in arms is not spending money alone. It is spending the sweat of its laborers, the genius of its scientists, the hopes of its children

The cost of one modern heavy bomber is this: a modern brick school in more than 30 cities. It is two electric power plants, each serving a town of 60,000 population. It is two fine, fully equipped hospitals. It is some fifty miles of concrete pavement.

We pay for a single fighter plane with a half million bushels of wheat. We pay for a single destroyer with new homes that could have housed more than 8,000 people.

This is, I repeat, the best way of life to be found on the road the world has been taking.

This is not a way of life at all, in any true sense. Under the cloud of threatening war, it is humanity hanging from a cross of iron."

—President Dwight D. Eisenhower, in "The Chance for Peace," his first formal address after becoming President[100]

On what date did Iraqi troops invade the United States? They didn't. No significant Iraqi attack preceded a U.S. decision to attack that country, overthrow the dictatorship of Saddam Hussein, and occupy Iraq for a time that has lasted longer than our entire involvement in World War II. American forces are now presiding over an endless religious civil war between Sunni and Shiite death squads. Instead of suppressing terrorism, we are creating terrorists.

The United States, with less than 5% of the world's population, accounts for nearly half of the world's military spending.[101] In looking for cuts in federal spending, unnecessary wars and excessive military spending are obvious places to cut and can produce large savings.

Stop the Iraq War Immediately

"How do you ask a man to be the last man to die for a mistake?"—John Kerry appearing before the Senate Foreign Relations Committee in 1971

The Iraq war serves no purpose worth the life of a single additional U.S. soldier. It is my fervent hope, writing in early 2007, that by the time you read this, we will have left Iraq and spared the lives of our soldiers.

Are we there to overthrow Saddam Hussein? We accomplished that in 2003. Are we there to secure weapons of mass destruction? Those weapons didn't exist. Are we there to fight a "global war on terror?" We've created a training ground for terrorists, where they can attack Americans without the considerable difficulties of infiltrating our homeland. Are we there because the Iraqis want us there? Seven out of ten Iraqis want us to leave within a year. Even more believe that our forces are causing more conflict than they are preventing. Are we there to protect a peaceful majority of Iraqis from the insurgents? 61% of Iraqis support the insurgent attacks![102] Are we there to protect a government that could not survive on its own? The government is controlled by the Shiites, who are nearly two thirds of the population and able to take care of themselves. Are we arming progressive and democratic forces? The new security forces are infiltrated by the insurgents; our arms and technologies go to murderers and religious fanatics.

To win the Iraq war would take much more than a surge of 21,500 more troops before a possible troop withdrawal in 2008. To win in Iraq would take conscription; 500,000 U.S. ground troops for several years; replacing Iraqi self-government with an American military government as we did in Japan after World War II; rebuilding the Iraqi economy from the ruins at our expense; securing Iraq's borders when we haven't been able to secure our own; and going house to house to disarm the entire Iraqi population who currently all have automatic weapons and easy access to unlimited quantities of explosives. To win in Iraq would also require spending trillions more dollars, in addition to the four hundred billion dollars that the war has already cost.

It is time to say simply: "Coalition forces long ago accomplished the missions of ending Saddam Hussein's dictatorship and the transition to a democratically elected Iraqi government. Establishing a secure and prosperous Iraqi nation is not the job of coalition forces but of the sovereign government and people of Iraq. Establishing and maintaining peaceful relations between religious and ethnic groups is not the job of coalition forces but of the sovereign government and people of Iraq. You have ample educated citizens and oil revenues to accomplish such goals. The coalition has already transferred tens of billions of dollars of aid to the new government. We're done here. All of our troops are leaving immediately. The flow of aid is stopping immediately. We are providing resettlement visas and assistance to some Iraqis and their families, those who worked with coalition forces and who may be in danger if they remain in Iraq. We look forward to maintaining normal, cordial relations with the sovereign government and people of Iraq. Good luck."

Stop the Iraq War Savings[103]

	Saved Each Year	Saved in a Lifetime
Per Person	$325	$26,000
Per Family	$1,300	$104,000
For Our Country	$97.5 billion	$7,800 billion
The Iraq war is unlikely to last for 80 more years, so the "saved in a lifetime" figures are what we save by avoiding this war and similar wars for that time.		

Keep Out of Civil Wars

""Everybody sees a difficulty in the question of relations between Arabs and Jews. But not everybody sees that there is no solution to this question. No solution! There is a gulf, and nothing can bridge it… We, as a nation, want this country to be ours; the Arabs, as a nation, want this country to be theirs."—David Ben-Gurion, later the first prime minister of Israel, in 1919[104]

In two dozen nations around the world, there are actual or potential civil wars between ethnic groups or factions desiring the same territory. There is generally no U.S. national interest served by getting involved in other groups' civil wars:

Israel/Palestine: The United States should stay out of this hundred-year-old conflict, saving more than $4 billion each year in aid to Israel and Egypt.[105] The United States began some of these subsidies after the 1978 Camp David accords, essentially bribing the parties to reach a peace agreement.

The fact that many Americans like Israel more than its enemies is immaterial; the fact that we cheered for Israel in its military victories over its neighbors is immaterial. No U.S. national interest is served by allying ourselves with a tiny Jewish state in a large Islamic region. Our main national interest in that part of the world is a secure oil supply for us and our allies. When Saddam Hussein threatened our oil supply and our Arab allies in 1990 by invading Kuwait, we assembled a coalition, went to war, and threw him out. Involvement with Israel has the opposite effect, of endangering our oil supply, as occurred in 1973 to 1974, when the Arab oil embargo begun during the Yom Kippur war quadrupled oil prices and triggered a recession.[106]

China/Taiwan: When the Chinese civil war ended in 1950, the communists controlled the mainland (People's Republic of China, PRC) and the anti-communists (nationalists) controlled the large island of Taiwan (Republic of China). The formerly communist PRC is now a largely capitalist country, often more capitalist than the United States, though still controlled by an authoritarian communist party. Taiwan is a democratic and capitalist country and friend of the United States. During the Cold War, there were geopolitical and military advantages to supporting Taiwan in its conflict with the communists. There are no such advantages now. It is time to repeal the Taiwan Relations Act of 1979, which implies that the United States might defend Taiwan in a war with China. Given our own history, in which the southern states were forcibly kept in the union during the Civil War, we would find it difficult to defend Taiwan's right to permanently secede from China, especially when both governments agreed for decades that there is only one China.

North Korea/South Korea: The defense of South Korea by the United States and the United Nations was noble and proper during the Korean War of 1950-1953. The great disappointment in that war was that we failed to liberate the North and win the war, after the loss of more than 33,000 U.S. combat troops. 54 years later, the South has twice the population and 27 times the economic output of the North, with much more advanced technology. The South is well able to defend itself from the North without U.S. troops stationed on South Korea's territory. South Korea is one of our most faithful allies. It could be in our national interest to continue to protect South Korea with our nuclear forces, so that South Korea does not build its own nuclear weapons to protect against the bombs already built by North Korea.

Shiite/Sunni: The ongoing civil war in Iraq is taking place between Shiite and Sunni militias. These two major groups within Islam have been divided since the seventh century, for more than 1,300 years. As an example of how long a religious civil war can last, Catholics and Protestants battled for more than a century in Europe, killing millions of people, until Europeans ended their religious wars at the Treaty of Westphalia in 1648.

This section does not propose direct savings, but staying out of civil wars would be a good part of a future U.S. policy of avoiding unnecessary wars.

Withdraw from Afghanistan

The Afghanistan War began shortly after the 9/11/2001 attack on the United States. Afghanistan's Taliban government sheltered Osama Bin Laden, who had attacked the United States. The U.S. and allied Afghan forces invaded, overthrew the Taliban, and took control of the country in a few months. Afghanistan now has an elected government and continues to fight a guerilla war against the Taliban, with the help of U.S. and allied forces.

The International Security Assistance Force in Afghanistan has 32,000 troops from 37 nations, including 12,000 from the U.S. An additional 8,000 U.S. troops operate under U.S. command. So there are about 20,000 U.S. troops and

20,000 allied troops, many from our NATO allies, in Afghanistan.[107]

The Afghanistan war is much more of a success than the Iraq war. It was justified by a real attack against the U.S.; it has had fewer casualties and much lower costs; it has had more success in establishing a successful government; it has gained and kept more support from a coalition of allies. Because the Iraq war has taken about seven times as many U.S. troops and about five times as much money, ending the Iraq war could provide more resources for the Afghanistan war if such resources would help.

There are still compelling reasons to consider, in consultation with our allies, withdrawing U.S. and allied forces from Afghanistan. To understand these reasons, suppose that 400,000 Islamic troops from 37 countries occupied the United States in support of a weak government. Then suppose that those troops and the weak government prohibited Americans from manufacturing cars, computers, software, and movies, or from growing corn or wheat. If a fundamentalist Christian militia fought the foreign occupiers and protected the corn growers and the car makers, that militia would get much support from the American people.

What Afghanistan produces is opium, more than six thousand tons of opium in the 2005-2006 growing season, 92% of the world's entire supply. Growing and selling opium provides about one third of Afghanistan's entire economic output and directly supports about 10% of the country's population.[108] Afghanistan's opium economy produces a greater share of that country's economic output than cars, computers, software, movies, corn, and wheat together produce in our country. Opium is a narcotic and is used to produce heroin, a more dangerous narcotic. If we want to pursue our foreign policy goal of a peaceful, moderate, and Taliban-free Afghanistan, we can't simultaneously make ourselves the enemies of one third of the Afghan economy. While coalition forces have avoided aggressive anti-opium efforts, opium eradication is the official policy of the Afghan government, the United States, and our allies.

Withdrawing from Afghanistan would allow the United States and its allies to sidestep the complete contradiction between suppressing opium production and allowing Afghanistan's economy to thrive. The most straightforward policy would be to acknowledge that controlling the use of narcotics should be done in the consuming nations without imposing burdens on the producing nations. The United States could buy the entire Afghan opium crop for a fraction of what we are spending on military operations, but this book does not suggest creating farm subsidies for Afghan opium farmers when it has already suggested eliminating farm subsidies for American farmers.

Afghanistan's reliance on opium is one reason we should consider withdrawing; the second reason is that the presence of foreign, largely Christian, troops is an inevitable irritant. If there were 400,000 Islamic troops occupying the U.S., then many unemployed and undereducated teenagers would be attracted to whatever radical militias fought the occupiers. More than half the Afghan population is under age 18, the unemployment rate is 40%, more than half the people live in poverty, and more than half the people are illiterate.[109] Afghanistan has a long history of fighting foreign occupiers, having fought three wars with the British and a long war to defeat Soviet occupation troops. Afghanistan is an Islamic nation occupied by largely Christian troops. These conditions stimulate resistance to foreign occupiers.

The third reason to withdraw from Afghanistan is as part of a greater strategy, one of non-intervention and non-interference in the Middle East, Central Asia, and the rest of the Islamic world. There are hypothetical circumstances that could require U.S. and allied involvement in the region, such as an Iranian military invasion of Kuwait and Saudi Arabia, or a major state-sponsored attack on us or our allies. There are no present real circumstances that require our continued involvement in the region. Our complete withdrawal from the Islamic world would eliminate major problems in relations between our cultures.

End the Afghanistan War Savings[110]

	Saved Each Year	Saved in a Lifetime
Per Person	$62	$4,960
Per Family	$248	$19,840
For Our Country	$18.6 billion	$1,488 billion
The Afghanistan war is unlikely to last for 80 more years, so the "saved in a lifetime" figures are what we save by avoiding similar wars for that time.		

Cut the Remaining Defense Budget by 50%

"At what point shall we expect the approach of danger? By what means shall we fortify against it? Shall we expect some transatlantic military giant, to step the Ocean, and crush us at a blow? Never! All the armies of Europe, Asia and Africa combined, with all the treasure of the earth (our own excepted) in their military chest; with a Buonaparte for a commander, could not by force, take a drink from the Ohio, or make a track on the Blue Ridge, in a trial of a thousand years.

At what point then is the approach of danger to be expected? I answer, if it ever reach us, it must spring up amongst us. It cannot come from abroad. If destruction be our lot, we must ourselves be its author and finisher. As a nation of freemen, we must live through all time, or die by suicide."

—Future President Abraham Lincoln's address to the Young Men's Lyceum in Springfield, IL on 27 January 1838.[111]

National defense is an essential and legitimate function of government. Unnecessary wars, policing the world, and wasteful spending are not essential. If we drastically cut the defense budget, who would attack us? Japan, Germany, Italy? These strong countries and former foes are all our friends and allies. Most of Europe, many countries of East Asia and the Pacific, Canada, and Latin America are all friendly towards us. We continue to support a vast military machine that faces no major threats. Russia threw out the communists in 1991 and now has a growing capitalist economy. China's "communist" party has embraced free market policies since 1978; China is now the world's most successful capitalist country.

Our military spending is six times China's spending and ten times Russia's spending. Our military spending is fifty times the combined spending of Iran and North Korea, the two remaining nations in the "axis of evil" identified by President Bush. [112] Of the top twenty nations ranked by military spending, other than the U.S., 14 are U.S. allies, four are friendly to the U.S., and two (China and Russia) are neither allies nor enemies.[113] Figure 7.1 compares military spending.

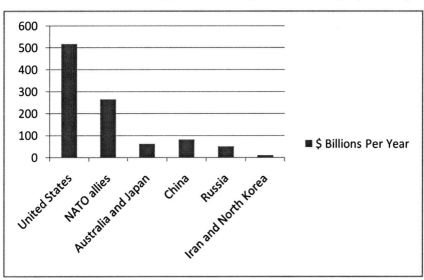

Figure 7.1. Relative Military Spending

During the Cold War our main enemies were the Soviet Union and China. One of the greatest surprises in recorded history was when the Soviet Union, armed to the teeth, peacefully dissolved into 15 separate nations, with Russia as the largest successor state. Russia is now a somewhat democratic and somewhat capitalist state with a strong government under President Vladimir Putin. Post-Soviet Russia has frequently meddled in the affairs of the other former Soviet republics, but has generally left the rest of the world alone. Russia has worked with the U.S. to reduce and control nuclear arms. Its population is less than half of the U.S. population, its economic output about one seventh of U.S. output, and its military relies on outdated equipment and short-term conscripts with low morale. Russia poses no current threat of world domination.

China is still officially communist and for 27 years was ruled by Mao Zedong, who sought the military strength to wage a world war against us. China under Mao was a real danger. China's current rulers are authoritarian but pragmatic, with no discernable desire to expand far beyond China's borders. If the United States stays out of a possible civil war between China and Taiwan, then there is no reason for our two nations to fight. China's economy is expanding rapidly, its restive people see the human rights enjoyed by other countries, and the main concern of China's leaders is internal control over 1.4 billion Chinese.

The 9/11 attack on America and other terrorists attacks abroad create legitimate concerns about military conflict with the Islamic world. The Islamic world is divided among dozens of different nations, some of them allied with the United States (Kuwait) and some antagonistic (Iran). The present U.S. military budget is eighty times what Iran spends each year and would still be forty times as much if we cut the military budget in half.[114] Iran may have an atomic bomb in a year and a few dozen bombs in several years. The United States has more than 5,000 active atomic and hydrogen bombs ready to launch. The U.S. could destroy Iran using only 1% of its nuclear weapons.

The main irritants in relations between the U.S. and Islamic countries are U.S. interventions in the region, including our needless and counter-productive involvements in Iraq and in the Israel/Palestine conflict. Some stateless terrorist networks like al-Qaeda will want to harm the United States even if we are not involved in the Islamic world. However U.S. non-involvement will greatly reduce the grievances of the Islamic population, reduce the ability of terrorists to recruit youngsters, and stop putting U.S. troops in the middle of terrorist populations where they are easy and accessible targets.

Our generals and admirals can work out the details; here are the broad outlines of how to cut military spending by 50%:

- *Cut by more than 50%*: Troops overseas, including those in South Korea, Europe, and other Middle East or Central Asian countries besides Iraq and Afghanistan.

- *Cut by more than 50%*: Subsidies for research and development, and money spent to buy very expensive new weapons systems.

- *Cut by more than 50%*: Classified government spending, including the Central Intelligence Agency, the National Security Agency, and the Defense Intelligence Agency. Much of what we need to know about other nations' military capabilities and intentions is now available from CNN, Google, and other public sources.

- *Cut by about 50%*: The strength and numbers in our regular armed forces, Air Force, Army, Marines, and Navy.

- *Cut by less than 50%*: National Guard and reserve forces. When these forces are not deployed for an ongoing war, they are much cheaper than active-duty forces per unit of war-fighting strength. The Iraq War has exhausted and demoralized these forces, citizen soldiers who have now become de facto regular front-line troops in an endless guerilla war.

- *Cut very little or not at all*: Our strategic nuclear forces, which are the best in the world and are a major reason that another country with strong conventional forces would still not want to attack us.

Cut the Remaining Defense Budget by 50% Savings[115]

	Saved Each Year	Saved in a Lifetime
Per Person	$676	$54,080
Per Family	$2,704	$216,320
For Our Country	$202.9 billion	$16,232 billion

There is ample precedent for big cuts in defense spending. From 1945 to 1948, military spending dropped from about $83 billion to about $9 billion, an 89% cut after World War II. Those cuts were probably too large and may have contributed to the subsequent Korean War because the communists saw our weakness. The cuts proposed in this chapter total $319 billion or 61% of our military spending, significant but much less severe than the cuts in 1945-48.

The cuts in this chapter are about 32% of our trillion dollar goal. Together with the cuts in the last chapter, we have now saved 46% of our goal.

8 RESTRAIN SOCIAL SECURITY AND MEDICARE

"Grow old along with me! The best is yet to be, the last of life, for which the first was made ..."—Robert Browning

The largest financial expense in the federal budget is taking care of old people, via Social Security Old Age and Survivors Insurance (OASI) payments and Medicare. Social Security began in 1935 under President Franklin Roosevelt with a combined tax rate of 2% on the first $3,000 of wages. Medicare, providing government medical insurance for those age 65 and over, began in 1965 under President Lyndon Johnson. Significant changes in Social Security were made in 1983 under President Reagan, changes recommended by a commission chaired by Alan Greenspan, later chairman of the Federal Reserve. Those changes included raising the normal retirement age from 65 to 67. Medicare expanded to included a major prescription drug benefit (Part D) in 2006, under President George W. Bush.

When government takes money from one group of people and gives that money to another group, most of us prefer that the money go to support those who cannot support themselves. For example, we prefer that our money go to provide basic subsistence for an honest and scholarly blind man with few assets, rather than to a wealthy corporation seeking undeserved subsidies. The phrase "deserving poor" is often used to describe the intended target of tax monies. By this measure, Social Security old age benefits and Medicare are more successful than many other federal programs. Old people are less employable than the rest of us and have less earned income. Some have accumulated sufficient assets, pensions, and children to not need added income, but for many of those relying on Social Security and Medicare these programs are the difference between a decent life and a life of wretched poverty. Because these programs are universal and not limited to the poor, they are also simpler to administer and don't excessively discourage added retirement savings. One can make a case for replacing these systems with better ones, but we should begin by acknowledging that these systems, especially Social Security old age benefits, are among the more successful programs of the federal government.

Social Security and Medicare are funded by the simplest, most straightforward, and burdensome income tax imposed by the U.S. government, a true "flat tax" on earned income, divided equally between employees and employers. The Social Security tax (including OASI and disability insurance, DI, or OASDI combined) is 12.4% of earnings up to a "cap" amount (Social Security wage base) adjusted annually, $97,500 per year in 2007. So a high earner pays 6.2% of $97,500 into Social Security, $6,045 per year, matched by an additional $6,045 per year from his or her employer. The Medicare tax is 2.9% of earnings with no cap, so the combined tax rate is 15.3% of earnings up to the Social Security wage base and 2.9% above that amount.

Social Security taxes have provided more money than is needed to pay benefits for many years. Those surpluses are deposited in Social Security's trust funds, invested in special U.S. Treasury debt. The surplus in tax revenue plus the substantial interest credited on the large trust fund balances was about $185 billion more than spending in FY 2006.[116] Those surpluses will keep increasing for several more years. The total OASDI trust fund balances were nearly $2 trillion at the end of 2006 and will increase to more than $4 trillion by 2016, enough to pay benefits for more than four years even with no new revenue.[117]

The Story of SecureTown

Once upon a time, there was a town that had gone through a lot. Back in '29 the economy had collapsed and a fourth of the town's men were unemployed by '33. Then came the big war in '41. Most of the men went to war for four years, the women left their homes to work in the war factories, and everybody just wanted peace, prosperity, and security when the war ended in '45. A year later the babies started coming, dozens then hundreds of babies in town; they called it a "baby boom." All those families and babies needed houses and schools and places to shop. There was new construction everywhere. The men who came home from the war all worked in the big auto parts factory at the edge of town. They could work there for thirty years, get a good pension, and retire well. The economy boomed and it seemed that anything was possible. Each Fourth of July, politicians spoke at the war veterans' cemetery and promised more and more security along with more prosperity for the town. The town changed its name to SecureTown.

Part of that security was a government pension for every worker, started back in '35 when the economy was still bad. Employees and employers each put in 1% of pay, for a total tax rate of 2%. The pensions were small and usually started at age 65, at a time when half of the town's men died before that age. In '50 the town had 1,000 men and women still working and 60 people, mostly men, receiving the new government pensions. There were 16 workers for every pensioner. The system was "pay as you go" and did not have large financial reserves. As more workers took their government pensions, the tax rates had to increase, doubling by '54, and tripling by '60, to 3% from employees and 3% from employers for a total tax rate of 6%. Still, life was good and it took the towns' citizens a long time to notice the changes happening around them.

One unnerving change was that their kids were different. They hadn't been through the really hard times like their parents. They didn't save money; they got into debt. There were new pills to prevent pregnancy; by the '70s the birth rate had dropped in half from the baby boom peak. These kids didn't care if they saved for retirement or if they had children of their own to take care of them. It was almost as if they thought the town was going to take care of them when they were old, which was more and more the case because of the town's government pensions.

The changes for old people were good. The poverty rate for old people dropped from one third to about 10% because of the new pensions. Old people were living longer as well, benefiting from both the security of their pensions and from new medical treatments. Some of those treatments were costly and a few old people used up their own savings and their kids' money paying for them. In '65 the town's mayor came up with the bright idea of having the town pay for old people's medical bills in addition to their government pensions, all paid for by another payroll tax that started small and then multiplied.

By the '80s the town's big auto parts factory was laying off workers. Our old war enemies overseas were building cheaper, better cars and cheaper parts. It wasn't a problem for the brighter young workers, who were working for the new computer companies starting up. The new companies didn't have the old-style pension plans; by the '90s even the auto parts factory ended its old pension. Instead workers had the new "401k" accounts, most invested in the stock market, most looking good until the big market crash in '00.

By '07 the town's people had mixed feelings about the government pensions and health care systems. There were 3,000 workers now, as the town had doubled in population in the last sixty years and many of the women in town had taken jobs. The number receiving government pensions had grown to more than 900, fifteen times as many as in 1950. Supported by government payments, there was a big new hospital in town and more doctors, but health care costs had multiplied. Spending on old age pensions and health care now took nearly one third of the town's budget. Both employers and employees hated the town payroll taxes, which now took more than 15% of the pay from the first dollar without exemptions, credits, or deductions. Many people paid more in payroll taxes than in personal income tax. Despite the high taxes, articles and pundits warned that the pension and health care systems weren't sound and could bankrupt the town in the future. All those babies born in the

'40s, '50s, and '60s had grown up and would start retiring next year; they didn't like the idea of any changes in their pensions or health care. Younger workers wondered whether they would ever receive any benefits from the systems, by the time they retired.

SecureTown's story is the U.S. story in miniature, of a town and a country now facing large liabilities for retiree pensions and health care.

Social Security's Future Financial Problems

"Beginning in 2017, Social Security will start using interest credits to meet full benefit obligations. The government will need to raise taxes, reduce benefits, increase borrowing from the public, and/or cut spending for other programs to meet its obligations to the trust fund."
—2006 Financial Report of the U.S. Government[118]

Social Security's large dedicated tax revenues and huge trust fund balances mean that there is no immediate financial problem for the system. There are still two large future financial problems related to Social Security.

First, Social Security's cash flow is negative beginning in 2017, with spending greater than dedicated tax revenues. This negative cash flow puts pressure on other parts of the federal budget and increases deficits unless we enact major federal spending cuts or tax increases. The trust funds will keep increasing for a few more years because of the large amounts of interest credited on their balances. Then Social

Security will need to cash in more bonds each year than the interest earned, reducing the trust fund balances.

Second, benefit payments will exceed dedicated tax revenues continuously and by so much that the main OASI trust fund will be exhausted by about 2041. Under current law, when the trust fund is exhausted then benefits are cut so that benefits are paid solely out of ongoing tax revenue, an estimated 25% cut in all benefit checks.[119]

Social Security's future financial problems have one major cause: people are living longer and drawing Social Security payments for many more years, increasing the number of beneficiaries relative to the size of the taxpaying work force. A national headline in April 2007 concerned Elsie McLean[120], an athletic 102-year old woman who hit a hole in one at the golf course. If Elsie started receiving Social Security at age 65, then she has been receiving payments for 37 years since 1970. Her athletic prowess and good health make it likely that Elsie will receive Social Security payments for many more years; we wish her good health and long life.

In 1950 there were 16 workers paying into Social Security for every one person receiving old age benefits; today there are just over three workers paying in for every person receiving old age benefits; in 2050 there will be only two workers paying in for each recipient, unless we make changes.

Several secondary factors worsen Social Security's future financial problems: the impending retirement of the large Baby Boom generation, lower birth rates, and declining labor force participation by older men (partly due to Social Security and other government programs). So much attention has been given to the retiring Baby Boomers that many analysts have over-emphasized their role in the problem. Currently each beneficiary is supported by the tax payments of 3.3 workers. When the Baby Boomers retire, the number of workers per beneficiary drops to 2.2 by 2030, a 50% increase in the relative burden on each worker.[121] The passing of the Baby Boom generation won't solve Social Security's problems. Because of longer life spans, the number of workers per beneficiary will continue to decline even after most Baby Boomers are dead.

> *Social Security's financial problems begin with the Baby Boom generation but will not end with that generation.*

The problem that begins with the Baby Boom generation is not the size of any particular generation, but our longer life spans and the greater portion of our lives spent receiving Social Security payments.

Raise the Social Security Retirement Age

In 1940, a worker at age 65 had 12 to 13 years of remaining life expectancy. In 2001, a worker at age 65 had 16 to 19 years of remaining life expectancy, an average of five more years of life.[122] The normal retirement age under Social Security was originally 65 and is now 67 for younger workers. To pay Social Security benefits for the same number of years to a retired worker as in 1940, the normal retirement age should be 70 or higher today, reflecting our longer lives and better medical technology. As described below, we should gradually increase the normal retirement age to 70 over a 24-year period from 2010 to 2033. Medical technology and life expectancy are both still improving rapidly, so this proposal increases the retirement age further to age 75 over a 30-year period from 2034 to 2063.

Figure 8.1 and Table 8.1 show how we should gradually raise both the normal retirement age and the early eligibility age for Social Security old age benefits, from the present ages of 67 and 62 to 75 and 65. Anyone born in 1948 or later would have a later normal retirement age than under current law. If these changes were enacted in 2008 or 2009, someone born in 1948 would have a year or two to adjust to a two-month delay before receiving the same early retirement benefits or normal retirement benefits. Those born in 1971 would have more than 20 years to adjust to a three-year delay in their Social Security retirement benefit. Children born in 2001 or later will have most of their life, fifty to sixty years, to adapt to retiring eight years later, in 2076 rather than 2068.

This proposal increases the normal retirement age beginning in 2010 and increases the early retirement age beginning in 2016. This proposal does not increase the early retirement age beyond age 65, but the increasing number of months between the normal and early retirement ages, with a reduction for each month that you retire early, will reduce benefits for workers who choose to retire at the earliest age. Social Security currently provides incentives and increased benefits for delaying retirement to age 70. It would be reasonable to increase this late retirement age to five years after the normal retirement age, to age 71 in 2010 increasing to age 80 by 2063.

Most of us in the Baby Boom generation (born 1946-1964) will be affected by these changes. For example, a worker born in 1953 will have to wait an extra year to receive full Social Security benefits. We Baby Boomers have run the federal government for the last 15 years, during which time that government has accumulated huge deficits in the Bush administration and failed to reform Social Security and Medicare in both the Clinton and Bush administrations. We should share in the costs of fixing these problems.

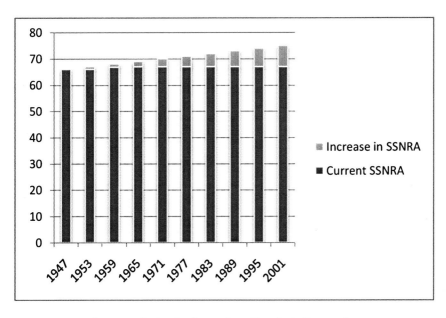

**Figure 8.1. Raise the Social Security
Normal Retirement Age
(Current and Increase by Birth Year)**

While future retirees will share in the cost of fixing Social Security, present retirees are held harmless and will actually benefit. Recall that without reform, the trust fund may be exhausted and benefit checks may be cut by 2041. The proposed reform will safeguard Social Security benefit checks for several additional decades.

Table 8.1. Increase Social Security Retirement Ages

Birth Year	Cur. SS Normal Ret. Age	New SS Normal Ret. Age	Current SS Early Ret. Age	New SS Early Ret. Age	Year Savings Begin *
		(Years + Months)			
1948	66	66+2	62	62	2010
1949	66	66+4	62	62	2011
1950	66	66+6	62	62	2012
1951	66	66+8	62	62	2013
1952	66	66+10	62	62	2014
1953	66	67	62	62	2015
1954	66	67+2	62	62+2	2016
1955	66+2	67+4	62	62+4	2017
1956	66+4	67+6	62	62+6	2018
1957	66+6	67+8	62	62+8	2019
1958	66+8	67+10	62	62+10	2020
1959	66+10	68	62	63	2021
1960 to 1965	67	68+2 to 69	62	63+2 to 64	2022 to 2027
1966 to 1971	67	69+2 to 70	62	64+2 to 65	2028 to 2033
1972 to 1977	67	70+2 to 71	62	65	2034 to 2039
1978 to 1983	67	71+2 to 72	62	65	2040 to 2045

* The increased number of months from early retirement to full retirement and increases in the full retirement age cause savings to begin when the affected population reaches age 62.

Table 8.1. Increase Social Security Retirement Ages (Continued)

Birth Year	Cur. SS Normal Ret. Age	New SS Normal Ret. Age	Current SS Early Ret. Age	New SS Early Ret. Age	Year Savings Begin *
		(Years + Months)			
1984 to 1989	67	72+2 to 73	62	65	2046 to 2051
1990 to 1995	67	73+2 to 74	62	65	2052 to 2057
1996 to 2000	67	74+2 to 74+10	62	65	2058 to 2062
2001 and later	67	75	62	65	2063
* The increased number of months from early retirement to full retirement and increases in the full retirement age cause savings to begin when the affected population reaches age 62.					

Adopting these increases in the retirement age will solve Social Security's financial problems for several decades.[123]

Raise the Social Security Retirement Age
Long-Term Savings
(Annualized Value of Future Savings)[124]

	Saved Each Year	Saved in a Lifetime
Per Person	$491	$39,280
Per Family	$1,964	$157,120
For Our Country	$147.2 billion	$11,776 billion
These figures use the annualized value of future savings, not immediate savings.		

Possible Social Security Changes Not Discussed

The George W. Bush administration has repeatedly proposed two changes in Social Security that are not discussed in depth here: (1) replacing wage indexing with price indexing in calculating initial Social Security benefits; (2) replacing part of Social Security with private investment accounts.

The administration's suggested change in indexing would reduce future Social Security benefits by up to half and reduce the portion of an average worker's income replaced by Social Security from 42% today to only 20% by 2075.[125] The proposed increase in the retirement age instead allows a worker to continue to replace a significant portion of their income through Social Security, by delaying retirement to the later retirement age.

The President's Commission to Strengthen Social Security (2001) recommended introducing private investment accounts as part of Social Security. However the proposed accounts would have received only a tiny part of Social Security taxes paid. The commission also proposed benefit cuts and increasing the progressivity of Social Security in some of its recommendations. The package never received serious political consideration. Social Security is already very progressive, giving six times as much benefit per dollar of wages earned to a low earner as to a high earner[126], a good reason to resist any changes that make the system more progressive.

For more than two decades the Cato Institute has made sound proposals for completely replacing Social Security retirement benefits with private investment accounts. Such accounts could eventually increase national savings, produce retirement benefits greater than Social Security, and be sustainable for the long run.[127] Such a change may be desirable but is outside the purpose of this book.

Medicare's Immediate and Worsening Financial Problems

As citizens and taxpayers, how would we react to a government promise to give a house to each person when they reach age 65? Someone retiring at age 65 in 2006 who lives another 19 years to age 84 will incur more than $240,000 in medical costs, almost all paid by Medicare.[128] In most areas of the United States we could buy a house for each Medicare beneficiary with that much money. When a married couple both go on Medicare, it is as if the taxpayers are buying them two houses. When nearly 80 million baby boomers go on Medicare between 2011 and 2028, their total Medicare costs will be in the tens of trillions of dollars.

Medicare has all of the major problems of Social Security plus three additional major problems. Like Social Security, the number of covered workers per covered beneficiary is dropping, beginning with the Baby Boomers' retirement and continuing thereafter. Unlike Social Security, Medicare has inadequate dedicated tax revenue compared to its spending and is already in deficit; has been expanded by Congress without major new revenue; and has open-ended costs that continue to grow.

A big government spending program doesn't require a dedicated tax; the Defense Department proves that. Medicare gets revenue from a Hospital Insurance (HI) tax of 2.9% (1.45% each from employee and employer) on all employment pay, about one fourth of Social Security's dedicated tax revenue of 12.4% of employment pay up to a ceiling ($97,500 in 2007). The other parts of Medicare, Supplementary Medical Insurance (SMI), are funded about one fourth by beneficiary premiums and about three fourths from the government's general revenues. SMI has a trust fund, but it operates more like your checking account, without a high balance as paychecks flow in and bill payments flow out. SMI takes money out of the government's general funds as needed. HI has a significant trust fund though much smaller than the Social Security trust fund. The HI trust fund is already spending more than it takes in and will be exhausted by about 2019. When HI spends more than it takes in, it redeems Treasury debt held by the trust fund, taking that money out of the general fund. When all of those trust fund assets are redeemed, Congress will need to either authorize direct transfers of general fund revenue (likely) or mandate severe cuts in payments to hospitals (unlikely).

In 2006, Medicare took $184.6 billion from the government's general revenues in addition to its dedicated revenues. By 2015 that amount will more than double to $395.4 billion.[129] In that same period total Medicare spending is projected to grow from $408.3 billion to $798.5 billion, nearly doubling in nine years.[130] Medicare is putting great pressure on the federal budget and is one of the major causes of our federal budget crisis.

Adding to that pressure since 2006 is a major expansion of Medicare, the new Part D drug benefit. If the government is going to cover medical expenses, it makes complete sense to cover medical drugs, which do more and more for us. However the new benefit was created without new tax revenues when the government was already running large deficits. President Bush proposed the new benefit in early 2003, promising that it would cost $400 billion over ten years. The Bush administration knowingly lied to get the bill passed and threatened to fire Medicare's chief actuary if he disclosed more accurate cost estimates. Two years later the estimated Part D cost had reached $720 billion, with estimated annual costs of over $100 billion by 2014.[131] Expanding Medicare may have helped Republicans in the 2004 elections, when their party gained seats in both the House and Senate. Any electoral benefit was short-lived, as voters angry at perceived mismanagement of the federal government, including high deficits, threw out the Republicans and gave control of both houses of Congress to the Democrats two years later in 2006.

Medicare's costs are open-ended because modern doctors are miracle workers, and miracles cost money. Today's health care professionals are much more effective than in past decades. Sixty years ago my young healthy uncle went to a good hospital for a hernia repair. He was dead a few days later, of a blood clot, because doctors then didn't guard against that complication as they do today. When I was young the boy across the street had an arm withered by polio, a disease now eliminated in most of the world. Today our surgeons are the world's best, doing more than a million heart surgeries each year, as well as transplanting organs, replacing hips and knees, and otherwise healing us so that we can have many more years of life and health. Our radiologists can scan our bodies to diagnose us without invasive procedures. Our pharmaceutical companies now make reliable medicines to lower our cholesterol, regulate our blood sugar, and prevent the lifestyle diseases of aging in America, like coronary artery disease and diabetes. Our public health agencies have made polio and smallpox footnotes in the history books. Health care is expensive and seems expensive to us, until we consider the alternatives of death or disability at an earlier age.

While we appreciate health care miracles, we also realize that those miracles are less and less affordable as national health care costs, many paid by government, approach two trillion dollars per year. Government's role in paying for health care and insulating us from the costs has greatly increased those costs.[132] The combination of Medicare, Medicaid, and private health insurance encouraged by our tax laws may have caused health care spending to double over the years.[133]

Make Medicare a High-Deductible Health Plan

Medicare is a complex, centrally planned, highly regulated health insurance program. Medicare is not just paying for major and catastrophic care, such as heart bypass surgery or cancer chemotherapy. Medicare pays more than one billion claims each year, about 23 claims per beneficiary.[134] Medicare pays for routine doctor visits, prescription drugs, lab tests, and other ongoing expenses for seniors who are not experiencing any major medical crisis.

To make real cuts in these huge costs, we should immediately transform all of Medicare, including the new prescription drug benefit, into a high deductible plan, where most beneficiaries must pay about 10% of their annual income as a deductible each year before receiving a dime from the government. A person with $10,000 income in the previous year would have a $1,000 annual deductible, one with $50,000 income would have a $5,000 deductible, etc.[135]

The high-deductible Medicare plan would be combined with health savings accounts (HSAs) which allow those in high-deductible health plans to pay deductibles or buy supplemental insurance with pre-tax dollars. Some seniors may buy supplemental insurance policies that cover the new high deductibles.

When we make Medicare a high-deductible health plan, Medicare Part D, the new drug benefit, should be revised to eliminate the bizarre feature known as the "donut hole." Currently Medicare covers $500 in drug costs above a $250 deductible, there is no coverage for annual drug costs from $750 to $3,600 (the "donut hole"), and Medicare Part D covers drug costs above $3,600. If Medicare becomes a high-deductible plan, there should be a combined deductible for all kinds of covered medical costs. Eliminating the coverage gap will cost $20.5 billion per year initially[136], reducing the high-deductible plan's savings.

Making such a big change in Medicare is also an opportunity to combine the multiple parts and multiple trust funds that now make up the program: Part A/HI (Hospitalization Insurance), Parts B and D/SMI (Supplemental Medical Insurance). Have seniors pay one premium for their cost sharing, remove some of the old restrictions in the HI program, and have one high annual deductible amount for all medical expenses. When the deductible amount is reached, there should be significant cost sharing, such as 20% of expenses incurred, until an out-of-pocket maximum amount of twice the deductible is reached.

The average income per person over age 65 in the U.S. is more than $23,300[137]. A poverty level income in the U.S. is about $9,800 per person.[138] To avoid drastic health cost increases for low-income seniors, the federal government would make an annual contribution of up to $800 to the HSA for low-income seniors. That contribution would phase out for incomes from $10,000 to $20,000, as shown in Figure 8.2 and Table 8.2.

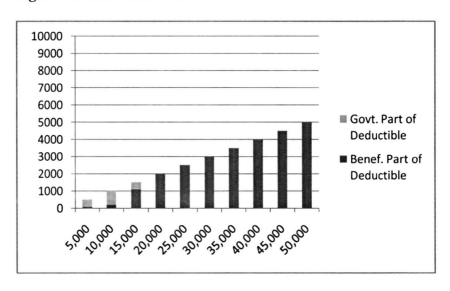

Figure 8.2. Medicare as a High-Deductible Health Plan (Annual Deductible vs. Annual Income)

Table 8.2. Medicare as a High-Deductible Health Plan

Annual Income	Annual Deductible	Federal Contribution	Beneficiary Contribution	Beneficiary Pct. of Income
$5,000	$500	$400	$100	2%
$10,000	$1,000	$800	$200	2%
$15,000	$1,500	$400	$1,100	7.3%
$20,000	$2,000	$0	$2,000	10%
$50,000	$5,000	$0	$5,000	10%
$100,000	$10,000	$0	$10,000	10%

Because HSA funds roll over from year to year, some incentives for economy in purchasing health care remain, even when bought with HSA funds.

The new high deductibles will save an average of $2,200 ($2,300 average new deductible minus $100 existing deductible) for each of 35.8 million Medicare beneficiaries age 65 and older, $78.8 billion per year. Some beneficiaries won't spend their high deductible amount each year, but some will spend beyond the deductible amount and incur up to twice the deductible in out-of-pocket costs in a year.

Providing federal HSA contributions averaging $500 each for 9 million seniors with incomes below 200% of poverty level will cost about $4.5 billion per year. Eliminating the coverage gap in the Medicare drug benefit will increase costs by $20.5 billion, producing net annual savings of $53.8 billion (78.8 - 4.5 - 20.5). Because of both increasing health costs per beneficiary and the increasing number of beneficiaries in coming years, annual savings should be much higher in future years.

Make Medicare a High-Deductible Health Plan
Higher Payments by Beneficiaries
Immediate Savings

	Saved Each Year	Saved in a Lifetime
Per Person	$179	$14,320
Per Family	$716	$57,280
For Our Country	$53.8 billion	$4,304 billion

The immediate savings just cited result from beneficiaries directly paying more of the costs of health care. There are two added and important effects that will noticeably reduce long-run Medicare costs. First, beneficiaries who are paying out of pocket or out of Health Savings Accounts avoid marginal and unnecessary medical spending, reducing medical spending. Second, when 36 million health consumers suddenly become more cost conscious and prudent health care consumers, that change creates significant downward pressure on health care prices. The savings from these two effects are not huge, estimated as a 5% reduction in future Medicare spending.[139] However projected future Medicare spending over the next 75 years is so large, with a present value of $52.6 trillion, that even a 5% reduction in that future spending is equivalent to annual savings of $76.3 billion.[140]

Make Medicare a High-Deductible Health Plan
Lower Health Care Spending Long-Term Savings
(Annualized Value of Future Savings)

	Saved Each Year	Saved in a Lifetime
Per Person	$254	$20,320
Per Family	$1,016	$81,280
For Our Country	$76.3 billion	$6,104 billion

Other Possible Medicare Savings

Medicare's huge costs and urgent financial problems make it especially important for us to lower those costs. If making Medicare a high-deductible health plan doesn't accomplish the needed long-term savings described in the last section, then here are two other ways to accomplish those savings:

- Encourage potential beneficiaries to delay enrolling in Medicare until they retire later under Social Security. Deposit some fraction of what Medicare is expected to cost, perhaps 30-50%, into the health savings accounts of those who continue to work past age 65 and delay receiving Social Security and Medicare. This proposal doesn't raise the Medicare eligibility age, but has a similar effect by encouraging people to delay enrolling in Medicare. The Congressional Budget Office analyzed one proposal to raise the Medicare eligibility age and found that it would reduce Medicare enrollment by about 17% and spending by about 9% a year.[141]

- Voluntarily move more Medicare beneficiaries into managed care plans, such as health maintenance organizations, that have incentives for efficiency and quality care, but not for overusing medical services. Because managed care can be more efficient, it can often have lower beneficiary deductibles or premiums. This chapter's major proposal to make traditional fee for service Medicare into a high-deductible plan will likely increase the number of beneficiaries in such plans, known variously as Part C, Medicare+Choice, or Medicare Advantage.

Legislators and policy analysts have suggested dozens of other possible Medicare reforms. Because Medicare costs are large and growing, there will need to be repeated efforts every few years to revise the program and control costs.

The two proposals in this chapter save $277.3 billion per year, $53.8 billion in immediate savings and $223.5 billion in the annualized value of long-term savings. Such long-term savings are less precise and harder to calculate than immediate savings. The main purpose of long-term savings in Social Security and Medicare is to put these programs on a much sounder financial basis and make them sustainable for much longer without a future budget crisis.

This chapter's cuts are about 28% of our trillion dollar goal. With cuts in earlier chapters, we have saved 74% of our goal.

9 END NON-ESSENTIAL PROGRAMS

*"... don't let good things crowd out those
that are essential."—Richard G. Scott*

In May 2003 a young American climber, Aron Ralston, was
pinned in a remote Utah canyon by a heavy boulder. After
five days, alone and nearing certain death from dehydration,
Ralston amputated his own trapped arm with a dull multi-
tool, saving his life.[142] Ralston still climbs mountains, and his
story is celebrated as an example of cool and courageous
behavior under pressure. He lost his arm and saved his life;
many others would have dithered and died.

Aron's story is good preparation for this chapter, which
suggests axing some of our favorite federal programs,
starting with NASA, which took us to the moon.

Sell NASA

*"Since Yuri Gagarin and Al Shepard's epoch flights in 1961,
all space missions have been flown only under large,
expensive government efforts. By contrast, our program
involves a few, dedicated individuals who are focused
entirely on making spaceflight affordable,"—Burt Rutan,
designer of the first private sub-orbital manned spaceship*

In early 2007 I bought an air ticket from Denver to San
Diego for $200, choosing from three airlines and nine

flights. Many Americans fly dozens of times a year; air travel is an essential part of our economy. Imagine instead that air travel is provided by a government agency. It provides one flight a month from Denver to San Diego and a ticket costs $20,000. There would be no significant air travel industry.

Costs matter tremendously. NASA, the National Aeronautics and Space Administration, is a very expensive and underachieving program that has long outlived its original purpose. In 1957 the Soviet Union launched the first satellite into space. Space technology was militarily important because of its use for missiles, satellites, and possibly orbital weapons systems. The prestige of being first in space was important to both the United States and the Soviet Union in their Cold War competition for the hearts and minds of the world's peoples. NASA was formed in 1958. In 1961, several weeks after the failed Bay of Pigs invasion of Cuba, President Kennedy made NASA a major part of the American experience for decades to come, declaring:

"I believe that this nation should commit itself to achieving the goal, before this decade is out, of landing a man on the moon and returning him safely to the earth. No single space project in this period will be more impressive to mankind, or more important for the long-range exploration of space; and none will be so difficult or expensive to accomplish."

In July 1969, Neil Armstrong and Buzz Aldrin landed on the Moon, the first humans to ever reach another world. Five more Apollo missions reached the moon in the following three years. NASA has sent no humans to the moon or beyond for more than three decades since.

What NASA has done is spend half a trillion dollars since 1972. That huge sum has developed one type of partially reusable launch vehicle, the Space Shuttle, and built six shuttles; partly constructed one tiny space station; put various satellites in orbit; and sent a few dozen robot probes through our solar system.

The "International Space Station" began more than twenty years ago as the U.S. "Space Station Freedom." The station was budgeted at $15.3 billion, costs multiplied, and the project was salvaged by bringing in other countries as partners, including Russia, Japan, Canada, Europe, and Brazil. This tiny structure, the size of a house, won't be complete until 2010, at a total construction cost of more than $100 billion. It currently supports a crew of three and will have space for six astronauts when finished. The cost of sustaining one astronaut in the space station is more than one billion dollars per year. No major science or technology breakthroughs have been produced and none are expected.

The Space Shuttle program has cost $145 billion through early 2005, more than $1.3 billion per launch, or $26,000 per pound of payload. 25,000 people work on the shuttle program. Delivering payload to orbit is hard; doing so with a partly reusable and fairly safe vehicle is harder. The shuttle is an impressive piece of technology that even NASA now considers obsolete. NASA can't produce the major reductions in launch costs needed to open up the space frontier.

Those cost reductions will come from the U.S. private companies now developing orbital vehicles and habitats, like Armadillo Aerospace, Bigelow Aerospace, and Blue Origin. These companies are risking their own funds, not the taxpayers'. Some of them will fail, as Rotary Rocket did in 2001. This vast new frontier of space, a frontier that many Americans have yearned for, needs great innovation and much lower costs before it opens up.

Selling NASA's assets should generate several billion dollars, which can be used for continued data gathering and support of ongoing multi-year space missions.[143]

Sell NASA Savings[144]

	Saved Each Year	Saved in a Lifetime
Per Person	$50	$4,000
Per Family	$200	$16,000
For Our Country	$15.1 billion	$1,208 billion

Leave Art and Media to the Free Market

The federal government spends about $640 million each year on the Corporation for Public Broadcasting (CPB, $400 million), National Endowment for the Arts (NEA, $99 million), and National Endowment for the Humanities (NEH, $141 million).[145]

The United States has the world's largest and most profitable arts, entertainment, and media industries. Competent artists, writers, and journalists not only thrive here but earn millions of dollars in the free market. The First Amendment to our Constitution, the cornerstone of our Bill of Rights, is about keeping government and free expression separate.

Public TV (PBS) is the most visible media affected by these proposed cuts. It is a haven for recycled British TV shows,

60s rock and roll specials encouraging donations in exchange for DVDs, and self-help infomercials encouraging donations in exchange for books, along with good documentaries and news shows. Many of us love public TV and it will continue without federal funding. Public TV gets much of its funding from the corporate community and from viewer pledges. Public TV gets significant advertising revenue from corporate sponsorships that put a company's name, tag line, and a brief video at the beginning or end of a PBS program.

Leave Art and Media to the Free Market Savings

	Saved Each Year	Saved in a Lifetime
Per Person	$2	$160
Per Family	$8	$640
For Our Country	$0.6 billion	$48 billion

End Federal Funding for Biomedical Research

The federal government has a vast bureaucracy for health research, the National Institutes of Health (NIH), comprising 19 institutes, 9 centers, and various other parts. NIH directly employs thousands of researchers and gives 50,000 grants each year to 325,000 researchers.[146] It pays for 28% of all U.S. biomedical research.[147] This huge amount of funding, equal to a Manhattan Project every year[148], does not produce enough medical breakthroughs to be worth the money spent. This amount of central government control over research is also inconsistent with the spirit of free minds conducting free inquiry in a free society. We should pull the plug on NIH.

Without federal funding, there will still be ample funding of health research by drug companies, biotechnology companies, medical device companies, foundations, and universities, totaling more than $72 billion per year.[149]

End Federal Funding for Biomedical Research Savings[150]

	Saved Each Year	Saved in a Lifetime
Per Person	$94	$7,520
Per Family	$376	$30,080
For Our Country	$28.2 billion	$2,256 billion

End Federal Funding for the National Science Foundation

The federal National Science Foundation (NSF) provides most federal funding for science other than medical science, including mathematics, computer science, physics, and the social sciences. These fields will all survive in our universities without federal subsidies.

NSF spends nearly a billion dollars each year to subsidize computer networking and information technology. These subsidies are a waste of money because the private companies in these fields are the most profitable in America and collectively spend more than forty billion dollars a year on research and development, forty times what the federal government spends.[151]

End Federal Funding for the National Science Foundation Savings[152]

	Saved Each Year	Saved in a Lifetime
Per Person	$18	$1,440
Per Family	$72	$5,760
For Our Country	$5.5 billion	$440 billion

Sell Amtrak

For decades our federal government has been trying to run a passenger railroad, and not doing it well. Selling Amtrak or ending its subsidies has long been suggested by budget reformers. The Government Accountability Office says that Amtrak's long-distance trains "show limited public benefit for dollars expended" and that "these routes account for 15 percent of riders but 80 percent of financial losses."[153] When we get government out of the rail business, passenger trains will still run in profitable corridors, such as the Northeast corridor from Washington D.C. to New York to Boston.

Sell Amtrak Savings[154]

	Saved Each Year	Saved in a Lifetime
Per Person	$3	$240
Per Family	$12	$960
For Our Country	$1.0 billion	$80 billion

The five proposals in this chapter save an immediate $50.4 billion each year, 5% of our trillion dollar goal. With the cuts in earlier chapters, we have now saved 79% of our goal.

10 RESTORE FEDERALISM

"The powers not delegated to the United States by the Constitution, nor prohibited by it to the States, are reserved to the States respectively, or to the people."—U.S. Constitution's Tenth Amendment, part of the Bill of Rights

Federalism is the reason that FBI agents don't give you traffic tickets, school teachers aren't federal employees, and the pothole on your street is fixed by the city, not the U.S. Department of Transportation.

Our federal government is a political union of state governments, the United States. The federal system divides sovereignty and responsibilities between the federal government and the state governments, in accordance with the U.S. Constitution. Each state has its own constitution and recognizes subordinate local governments, such as cities, counties, and special districts.

The Constitutional division of powers between the federal and state governments lists specific powers for the federal government, mainly the control of foreign and military affairs, along with certain areas where uniformity between the states was sought, such as coinage, patents, post offices, and the regulation of interstate commerce. The federal government has since expanded into many areas not listed in the Constitution, but considered constitutional by the courts, such as Social Security, Medicare, and economic regulation.

Past expansion of federal power relative to the states was reasonable, because the Southern states did not protect the rights of many of their citizens for many years. When the United States began, white southerners enslaved black (African-American) southerners and asserted the right to do so permanently. The bloodiest war in U.S. history, the Civil War, freed the slaves and officially gave them political rights. The rights of blacks were suppressed again for another century, through a combination of segregation (discrimination institutionalized in state and local laws) and white terrorism against blacks carried out by the Klu Klux Klan and other white citizens groups. This American apartheid against blacks persisted into the 1960s.

Thankfully times have changed. Since the 1960s, blacks in the South and nationally have achieved their rightful share of political power. There are now more than 4,000 black elected officials in the Southern states. In the Southwestern states, from Texas to California, Hispanic officeholders are prominent in state and local governments, overcoming decades of prejudice. In the 2008 Presidential race, black and Hispanic candidates are prominent. Racism has not disappeared in the United States, but we no longer need centrally controlled federal programs to overcome resistance from state governments controlled by bigots.

This chapter suggests that the federal government stop providing funds, and stop issuing mandates for how funds are used, in several areas that are primarily state and local government responsibilities. Each of the fifty states has a large government and economy that can handle its responsibilities. Our most populous state, California, has more people and economic output than Canada. A less populated U.S. state, like Vermont or Wyoming, still has more people and a greater economic output than a well-run small foreign nation, like Belize or Iceland.[155]

End Most Federal Education Programs

Does a dollar grow if it is sent on a six thousand mile round trip? I asked Oregon citizens that question years ago, when promoting education reform. Oregon sends tens of billions of dollars of tax money each year to the federal government in Washington, D.C., three thousand miles away. Oregon receives back a few hundred million dollars of federal money for K-12 education. While the state spends nearly half of its budget on education, the federal government spends three percent of its budget on education, one sixteenth as much. The best way to have money for education is to keep the money at the state and local level, or in the hands of parents, and not send it to the federal government.

Federal money for K-12 education also comes with mandates and regulations that may cost more than the money received. According to the American Federation of Teachers, mandates in one area, special education, cost more than $40 billion per year[156], which is greater than federal funding for special ed.

We should eliminate most federal education programs, moving one program (Pell grants for low-income students) to the Department of Health and Human Services so that we can shut down the federal Department of Education. Loan programs were already cut in chapter 3. The remaining federal education spending to cut is about two thirds for K-12 education and one third for college education.[157]

All sorts of education will continue to thrive without federal subsidies. The United States spent more than $800 billion dollars on education in 2004, more than $500 billion on K-12 education and more than $300 billion on college education.[158] The cuts proposed in this chapter are less than 6% of national spending on each kind of education.

End Most Federal Education Programs Savings[159]

	Saved Each Year	Saved in a Lifetime
Per Person	$159	$12,720
Per Family	$636	$50,880
For Our Country	$47.8 billion	$3,824 billion
Excludes Pell Grants for low-income college students, which are kept. Excludes student loan funding which is cut in Chapter 6.		

End Many Grants to State and Local Governments

With each U.S. state the size of a nation, total spending by state and local governments is significant, more than two trillion dollars per year. Money from the federal government is about one fifth of state and local spending.[160] All the proposals in this chapter cut less than half of all federal grants to state and local governments, or less than 10% of their total spending in cuts.

This section proposes ending many grants to state and local governments as shown in Table 10.1, about one fourth of total grants. This section combined with the previous section cuts about one third of total grants. Cuts in other chapters, like ending farm programs, also cut some grant money.

Table 10.1. Cuts in Other Grants to State and Local Governments[161]

Grant Area	Cut (Billions)
Energy	0.7
Natural resources and environment	5.9
Commerce	1.5
Transportation (except core highway and airport grants)	9.3
Community and regional development	8.6
Education, training, employment, and social services (excluding the Department of Education, cut elsewhere in this chapter)	20.4
Health	8.1
Income security	33.7
Administration of justice	3.7
General government	1.5
Total	**93.4**

While state and local governments will lose less than 10% of their total budgets, these cuts will still be difficult. Most states have balanced budget requirements in their state constitutions and several also have tax limits or spending limits. If states with such limits raise their taxes and spending to make up for lost federal money, then they will need approval from voters.

Grants to state and local governments or payments to low-income individuals (which reduce the welfare burden on state and local governments) that remain will include

Medicaid (as a block grant with future growth limited), core highway and airport grants, food stamps, WIC (women, infants, children) nutritional assistance, unemployment benefits, SSI (supplemental security income), Social Security disability and survivors benefits, tenant rental assistance, Pell grants for college, and TANF (temporary assistance to needy families).

End Many Grants to State and Local Government Savings

	Saved Each Year	Saved in a Lifetime
Per Person	$311	$24,880
Per Family	$1,244	$99,520
For Our Country	$93.4 billion	$7,472 billion

How Medicaid Endangers the Federal Budget

"On average, 57% of Medicaid funding comes from the federal government ... The more a state spends on its Medicaid program, the more it receives from the federal government. States can make their Medicaid benefits more generous than the federal government requires and can also extend eligibility to more people than the federal government requires."
—*Cato Handbook on Policy 6th Edition*

Since 1965 the federal government has provided money to the states to pay for health care for poor people, called Medicaid. A related program, the State Children's Health Insurance Program (SCHIP) was added in 1997. All references to Medicaid in this book include SCHIP spending. Federal Medicaid spending was $186.1 billion in FY 2006. Medicaid now covers more than 49 million people.[162]

Medicaid spending exploded from the beginning and continues to grow rapidly. Total Medicaid spending (not adjusted for inflation) grew five-fold from 1970 to 1980, nearly tripled from 1980 to 1990, nearly tripled again from 1990 to 2000, and will more than double from 2000 to 2010.[163] Figure 10.1 shows projected federal spending on Medicaid. Medicaid's present design contains two major incentives for more spending, its benefits package and its matching formulas.

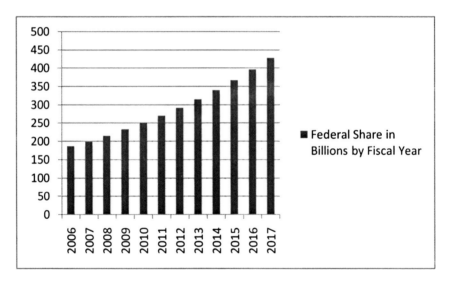

Figure 10.1. Projected Federal Medicaid and SCHIP Spending

First, Medicaid mandates an extremely generous benefits package that includes hospitalization, nursing and nursing homes, home health care, drugs, doctors, and dentists. Medicaid plans vary somewhat from state to state but generally have almost no copays or deductibles, so nothing prevents massive overconsumption of medical services. Medicaid benefits are more generous than Medicare and more generous than plans at many profitable U.S. corporations, which now impose high deductibles of thousands of dollars on their employees.

Second, when a state government spends an extra dollar on Medicaid, it gets an additional dollar or more from the federal government, according to a "federal medical assistance percentage" that varies from state to state. In Arkansas or West Virginia, each added state dollar is matched by about three added federal dollars, a huge incentive for state overspending. On average each added state dollar adds $1.33 from the federal government.[164] Medicaid spends hundreds of billions of dollars and is a huge part of state budgets, so there are large incentives for states to increase their federal Medicaid matching funds. For example, some states impose special taxes on health care providers, currently limited to 6% by Congress. The provider taxes add to the medical costs shared by the federal government while all the tax revenue goes to the states. This one gimmick adds about two billion dollars a year to federal Medicaid spending.[165]

Make Medicaid a Block Grant

We can fix Medicaid's main problems with one major change: replace all federal Medicaid spending with unrestricted block grants to the states, allowing the size of those grants to grow as our national economy grows. The block grant idea is not new; it was proposed by the Reagan administration in 1981, in the Congress in 1995, and again by the George W. Bush administration in 2003.[166]

With Medicaid as an unrestricted health care block grant, states can use the money for any health care spending or insurance. Depositing money into beneficiary's Health Savings Accounts should also be allowed. This reform completely eliminates any incentive for states to overspend. State tax funds are no longer matched by federal funds, but must compete with other state priorities, such as roads, prisons, and education.

This reform creates complete liberty for states to create better and more economical health care assistance systems. For example, a state may choose to eliminate health insurance mandates that raise insurance costs and then simply subsidize the purchase of basic health insurance for those who are poor but don't have major and chronic health problems. A state could get the economic advantages of high deductible health plans even for low-income beneficiaries by making significant initial deposits into Health Savings Accounts (HSAs) for such beneficiaries. Innovation is especially needed for long-term care, which now absorbs one third of Medicaid spending. States can move more quickly than the federal government to support home-based care and other alternatives that are much cheaper than government-paid nursing home care.

When we convert Medicaid to a block grant, we assume that the block grant begins by giving the states the same amount of money that Medicaid now provides. The substantial future savings are because the Medicaid block grant will grow much more slowly than Medicaid would otherwise grow. The nature of these projections is that both total and annualized savings grow substantially as you project for more years. For example, the annualized present value of Medicaid savings is $30 billion if we look 10 years ahead and $139 billion if we look 45 years ahead. Some other projections used in this book, for Social Security and Medicare, look 75 years ahead, because the Social Security and Medicare trustees use 75-year projections. For Medicaid savings, we are more conservative, using savings looking ahead just 25 years, an annualized present value of about $86 billion per year.

Make Medicaid a Block Grant Long-Term Savings (Annualized Value of Future Savings)[167]

	Saved Each Year	Saved in a Lifetime
Per Person	$286	$22,880
Per Family	$1,144	$91,520
For Our Country	$85.9 billion	$6,872 billion
These figures use the annualized value of future savings, not immediate savings. This proposal's savings are over a 25-year period; annualized savings are less for a shorter period and greater for a longer period.		

The three proposals in this chapter save $227.1 billion per year, $141.2 billion in immediate savings and $85.9 billion in the annualized value of long-term savings. This chapter's cuts are about 23% of our trillion dollar goal. With cuts in the earlier chapters, we have now saved 102% of our goal.

As described in the next chapter, our trillion dollars a year in budget savings will produce a substantial bonus, paying off federal debt held by the public.

11 CONSEQUENCES

"Sooner or later everyone sits down to a banquet of consequences."—Robert Louis Stevenson

The proposals made in the last five chapters will save us more than one trillion dollars each year, $710 billion in immediate savings and $309 billion as the present value of future savings that are achieved gradually, in Medicaid, Medicare, and Social Security. This chapter describes what we will lose, what won't change, and a big bonus: paying off the national debt held by the public.

Federal Government Services That We Will Lose

"No gains without pains."—Benjamin Franklin in Poor Richard's Almanack

Subsidies, pork and earmarks, corporate welfare, and farm programs will disappear. Some farmers and businesses that rely on government will go broke. Most farmers don't accept subsidies and will benefit. Giveaways to foreign governments will end, other than our required dues to the United Nations and other international organizations.

The federal government will no longer loan you money, subsidize a lower interest rate for your loan, or cosign your loan. The biggest group affected will be college students relying on student loans. Medical students may pay more for their education without federal subsidies.

Cities and states hit by major natural disasters will no longer get tens of billions of dollars in long-term federal aid. Rebuilding will be a state and local problem. The federal government will no longer write you a check if you build a house on the beach and a hurricane sweeps it away.

We will no longer be at war in Iraq and Afghanistan. Soldiers won't be dying in these countries. Military spending will be much less; many military employees and employees of military contractors will lose their jobs. Some military bases will close, affecting nearby communities.

If you are already receiving Social Security nothing will change. If you are in your fifties, you will wait several more months to receive Social Security. If you are in your thirties, you will wait three more years, until about age 70. If you are a young child, you will wait eight more years, until age 75.

If you are receiving Medicare then you will start paying a significant deductible of 10% of your annual income, along with significant copayments that could make your out of pocket medical costs reach 20% of your annual income. You will be free to buy extra insurance to cover these costs, but if you are very old or in bad health then extra insurance won't be affordable. The federal government will contribute some money to Health Savings Accounts for low-income seniors.

The Chinese government may send astronauts to the Moon in a few years, along with the Japanese, Indians, and Russians. The next U.S. astronauts on the Moon or anywhere else will work for private companies. NASA, the Space Shuttle, and the International Space Station will all be sold.

Your local public broadcasting station will solicit more donations and run more ads after losing federal funds. If the opera company or museum in your city now receives federal money, it may cut shows or raise prices.

There will be less medical and scientific research in colleges and universities. Researchers losing grants will seek support from companies and foundations.

State and local governments will lose significant amounts of federal money, but will also be free of the federal mandates that come with that money. There will be no federal money for K-12 education and also none of the federal rules that have complicated K-12 education. Federal Medicaid funding won't grow as quickly, but states will have complete control of their own Medicaid programs.

Federal Government Services That We Will Keep

The federal regulatory state will be intact, the myriad of agencies that control and regulate our lives, such as FCC, FDA, OSHA, and SEC.

Core federal welfare programs that help low-income Americans are untouched: unemployment benefits, Social Security disability, Supplemental Security Income (SSI), Temporary Assistance to Needy Families (TANF), tenant rental assistance, food stamps, and WIC nutrition assistance. Medicaid spending will grow more slowly but will still grow, with complete flexibility for states to change and improve their Medicaid programs.

We will still have the largest military budget in the world. Instead of the United States alone having about half of all world military spending, the U.S. and our allies together will have about half of all world military spending.

Social Security and Medicare will still be there for older Americans, with later retirement for future Social Security recipients and much higher out-of-pocket health costs.

Environmental programs, federal lands, and the national parks will still be there, with the only cuts being in grants to state and local governments.

The apparatus of general government will be intact: the White House, Congress, the courts, and the other agencies that keep government functioning.

Some federal employees in affected agencies and departments will lose their jobs. This book does not propose any changes in pay or retirement benefits for the majority of federal employees who will keep their jobs.

Surveying a Smaller Federal Government

Table 11.1 describes how this book's cuts may affect federal cabinet departments. What is most important is to make needed cuts, independent of what department or agency contains a program. This book recommends ending most spending in four departments: Agriculture, Education,

Energy, and Housing and Urban Development (HUD). If we abolish those departments then any remaining programs from them can be moved to other departments.

This book's proposed cuts significantly affect six of the remaining eleven cabinet departments: Commerce, Defense, Health and Human Services, Homeland Security, State, and Transportation. Five departments are little changed by these cuts: Interior, Justice, Labor, Treasury, and Veterans Affairs.

Table 11.1. Impact of Cuts on Federal Cabinet Departments

Department	Impact
Agriculture	Abolish. Move food stamps and WIC nutrition programs to HHS. Move Forest Service to Interior Dept.
Commerce	Lose grant programs and corporate welfare. Gain some programs from Energy Dept.
Defense	Withdraw from Afghanistan, Iraq, and many overseas bases, ending war spending. Cut remaining spending 50%.
Education	Abolish. Move Pell Grants to HHS.
Energy	Abolish. Move Strategic Petroleum Reserve and regulatory functions to Commerce Dept.
Health and Human Services (HHS)	Gain some programs from Agriculture Dept., Education Dept., and HUD. Lose many grant programs, some Medicare spending, and the National Institutes of Health. Medicaid becomes block grants.
Homeland Security	Lose grant programs and Federal Emergency Management Agency (FEMA), which is abolished. Other programs are unchanged.

Table 11.1. Impact of Cuts on Federal Cabinet Departments (Continued)

Department	Impact
Housing and Urban Development	Abolish. Move rental assistance to HHS.
Interior	Lose grant programs. Gain Forest Service from Agriculture Dept. Largely unchanged.
Justice	Lose grant programs. Largely unchanged.
Labor	Lose grant programs. Largely unchanged.
State	Lose foreign aid programs.
Transportation	Lose Amtrak, many grant programs, and corporate welfare programs. Keep core grant programs for airports and highways.
Treasury	No major changes.
Veterans Affairs	No major changes.

Figure 11.1 shows how this book's cuts may affect other federal agencies. The abolition of some obscure agencies can be inferred from this book's cuts even when not explicitly specified. For example, ending foreign aid logically implies that the federal government would no longer contain a U.S. Agency for International Development.

Legislative Branch: The Congress, Senate, House of Representatives, Architect of the Capitol, Congressional Budget Office, Government Accountability Office, Government Printing Office, Library of Congress, United States Botanical Garden

Executive Branch: The President, The Vice President, Executive Office of the President, Council of Economic Advisors, Council on Environmental Quality, National Security Council, Office of Administration, Office of Management and Budget, Office of National Drug Control Policy, Office of Policy Development, Office of Science and Technology Policy, Office of the U.S. Trade Representative, Office of the Vice President, White House Office

Judicial Branch: The Supreme Court of the United States, United States Courts of Appeals, Administrative Office of the United States Courts, Federal Judicial Center, Territorial Courts, United States Court of Appeals for the Armed Forces, United States Court of Appeals for Veterans Claims, United States Court of Federal Claims, United States Court of International Trade, United States District Courts, United States Sentencing Commission, United States Tax Court

Independent Agencies and Government Corporations: *African Development Foundation, Broadcasting Board of Governors,* **Central Intelligence Agency,** Commodity Futures Trading Commission, Consumer Product Safety Commission, *Corporation for National and Community Service, Corporation for Public Broadcasting,* Defense Nuclear Facilities Safety Board, **Environmental Protection Agency,** Equal Employment Opportunity Commission, *Export-Import Bank of the U.S., Farm Credit System Insurance Corporation,* Federal Communications Commission, Federal Deposit Insurance Corporation, Federal Election Commission, *Federal Housing Finance Board,* Federal Labor Relations Authority, Federal Maritime Commission, Federal Mediation and Conciliation Service, Federal Mine Safety and Health Review Commission, Federal Reserve System, Federal Retirement Thrift Investment Board, Federal Trade Commission, General Services Administration, *Inter-American Foundation, Institute of Museum and Library Services,* Merit Systems Protection Board, *National Aeronautics and Space Administration,* National Archives and Records Administration, National Capital Planning Commission, National Credit Union Administration, *National Endowment for the Arts, National Endowment for the Humanities,* National Labor Relations Board, National Mediation Board, *National Railroad Passenger Corporation (Amtrak), National Science Foundation,* National Transportation Safety Board, Nuclear Regulatory Commission, Occupational Safety and Health Review Commission, **Office of the Director of National Intelligence,** Office of Government Ethics, Office of Personnel Management, Office of Special Counsel, *Overseas Private Investment Corporation, Peace Corps,* Pension Benefit Guaranty Corporation, Postal Rate Commission, Railroad Retirement Board, Securities and Exchange Commission, Selective Service System, *Small Business Administration,* Social Security Administration, Tennessee Valley Authority, *Trade and Development Agency, U.S. Agency for International Development,* U.S. Commission on Civil Rights, U.S. International Trade Commission, U.S. Postal Service

Figure 11.1. Impact of Cuts on Other Federal Organizations (*Italics* = abolished; bold = cut)[168]

Of 94 federal organizations outside of the 15 cabinet departments, this book's proposals abolish 19, cut three, and leave 72 unchanged. In the Environmental Protection Agency, grants to state and local governments are eliminated but core programs are not affected. The Central Intelligence

Agency (CIA) and the Office of the Director of National Intelligence are cut as part of cutting defense spending.

The three largest independent agencies abolished are the National Aeronautics and Space Administration (NASA), National Science Foundation (NSF), and Small Business Administration (SBA).

Pay Down the National Debt

These large savings and the associated sacrifices can produce a major national bonus, paying off that part of the national debt that is held by the public. Our emotional response to our national debt is a mix of hopelessness and intimidation; we are intimidated by the debt's huge size and feel hopeless that it will ever be paid. Things rarely remain the same. A huge debt that is not paid off is likely to grow to the point of bankruptcy, of default on debt, default on benefit promises, or hyperinflation when a nation is deep in debt.

What is amazing is how quickly we can pay off our external debt if we make the painful changes described in this book. The $710 billion of immediate cuts proposed are based on FY 2006 spending, or 5.4% of GDP for that year. By FY 2012, cuts of 5.4% of GDP will be $960 billion.

Figure 11.2 shows how quickly we can pay off our debt assuming that this book's immediate savings are completely adopted by FY 2012 (1.1% of GDP saved in FY 2009, 2.7% in FY 2010, 4.4% of GDP in FY 2011, and 5.4% of GDP in FY 2012 and later). Long-term savings of 2.4% of GDP are phased in at 0.1% every two years over 48 years.

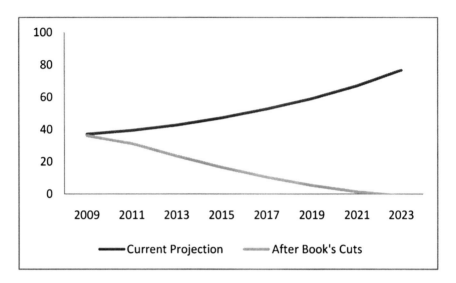

Figure 11.2. Paying Down Debt Held by the Public (% of GDP)

If we adopt this book's recommendations beginning when the 111th U.S. Congress convenes on 3 January 2009, then the public debt of the United States might be paid off by 30 September 2022, the last day of fiscal year 2022 and less than 14 years later. The mathematics of paying off the debt is straightforward; we must say "might" because we cannot predict our nation's exact future for the next two decades.

The difference in our nation's financial future is huge. On our current course we could have an FY 2022 deficit approaching two trillion dollars and public debt exceeding $20 trillion. By adopting all of this book's cuts we could have budget surpluses beginning in FY 2010 and have zero public debt by the end of FY 2022.[169]

The annualized value of paying off the federal public debt is less than FY 2006 net interest paid of $227 billion because it uses a real interest rate of 2.9%, which excludes inflation.

Pay Off Debt Held by the Public
(Annualized Value of Future Savings)

	Saved Each Year	Saved in a Lifetime
Per Person	$467	$37,360
Per Family	$1,868	$149,440
For Our Country	$140.0 billion *	$11,200 billion
* End of FY 2006 federal debt held by the public of $4,829 billion times a real interest rate of 2.9%.		

The total savings in Chapters 6 to 11 are $1,159.6 billion per year, 116% of our trillion dollar goal.

12 WHAT IS TO BE DONE?

"The ultimate test of a moral society is the kind of world it leaves to its children."—Dietrich Bonhoeffer

This chapter[170] describes how we can change our government so that fiscal balance is normal and not exceptional.

Change What We Ask from Our Politicians

"Politicians who vote huge expenditures to alleviate problems get reelected; those who propose structural changes to prevent problems get early retirement."—McClaughry's Law of Public Policy by John McClaughry[171]

Many of our politicians are decent hard-working people, doing an often thankless job. How our politicians act and vote generally reflects what the voters want; a politician is our representative and will not be reelected if he or she strays too far from our wishes.

For many years our politicians have had the luxury of pleasing every interest and voter group with a three-part formula for success and reelection: (1) increase spending on just about everything, (2) lower taxes or don't raise them, (3) cover the difference with borrowed money and unfunded future promises. We the voters have collectively enjoyed the spending programs, appreciated our lower taxes, and been willing to ignore the future bills.

As described in this book, times are changing and the old formula won't work much longer. Our elected officials will follow our lead. Here is what we need to start asking federal politicians and candidates at every opportunity:

- What will you do about the trillion dollar imbalance in the federal budget?

- How will we either change or pay for Social Security and Medicare?

- Should we focus on tax increases or spending cuts to fix the federal budget?

- What specific federal spending cuts or specific federal tax increases do you support?

- (If the candidate proposes new spending programs): How are you going to pay for the new programs you propose?

- (If the candidate proposes new or extended tax cuts): How are you going to pay for the tax cuts you propose?

- What legislative or constitutional changes do you support to help keep the federal budget balanced?

This book's proposed changes will be painful and opposed by powerful interest groups. Politicians will make such changes only when popular support for change outweighs the votes and contributions of those groups.

2008: an Opportunity for Change

This book is about policy not politics, but policies are only adopted if our politicians consent. Elections are opportunities for us to pressure our politicians, give them guidance, and exchange them for different politicians if needed. In 2008 we elect a President, Vice President, all 435 voting members[172] of the U.S. House of Representatives, and one third of the U.S. Senate.

Whether supporting these proposals or alternative proposals it would be useful if fiscal balance caucuses formed in all of our political parties, especially the Democratic and Republican parties, which select most elected officials.

For the election in 2008 or any other year to begin a major shift towards fiscal balance will require greater concern and knowledge about these issues at the grassroots, among the American people in general. The rest of this chapter assumes that we do elect a Congress and President that adopt this book's proposals and then work to make fiscal balance permanent. Call this hypothetical administration the GUTS party: Get Us To Surplus, eliminating the federal deficit and starting to pay down the debt.

The Turmoil of Change

This book's proposals are simple; legislation to implement them could be drafted in a few weeks. If we elect the GUTS candidates on 4 November 2008, the initial response of the media and various pressure groups will be: "They don't mean it." The next response will be "How dare they!" from various interest groups and well-meaning citizens who disagree.

By quick legislation, such as the impoundment power suggested in this chapter, significant government savings can begin in the first months after GUTS candidates take office. As programs are cut and subsidies stop, we can expect waves of organized public protest from various groups. As some farmers and businesses go broke and some government employees lose their jobs, we could have temporary increases in unemployment and a slow year for our economy.

If the GUTS program moves ahead and is largely implemented by the next elections in 2010, then its supporters will likely be reelected, as the federal deficit will be erased, paying down the debt will have begun, and business confidence will have increased.

The final part of the GUTS plan, described in the rest of this chapter, is to change how we manage federal finances so that fiscal balance is the norm rather than the exception.

Add a Balanced Budget Amendment to Our Constitution

"I wish it were possible to obtain a single amendment to our Constitution. ... I mean an additional article taking from the Federal Government the power of borrowing."
—Thomas Jefferson writing in 1798

Our federal Constitution cannot and should not be amended lightly. Twenty-seven amendments have been adopted in 218 years of government under the Constitution, all by a two thirds vote of each House of Congress followed by the approval of three fourths of the states. The Constitution specifies an alternate way to amend the Constitution, by convening a new Constitutional Convention at the request of two thirds of the states, which proposes amendments that must then be approved by three fourths of the states to take effect.[173] Since the repeal of Prohibition in 1933, no amendment has had a major impact on the American people or our system of government. The balance between the possibility of amendments and the difficulty of amendments is one of our Constitution's successes.

Requiring a balanced federal budget provides a good reason to amend the Constitution: a major national problem that cannot be solved by legislation but requires a Constitutional constraint. Our Congress generally legislates by simple majority. One Congress can enact rules to limit spending, and deficits and a later Congress can easily revise or repeal those rules. Congress passed spending limits in 1985 (Gramm-Rudman-Hollings) and 1990 (PAYGO). Both limits were later repealed. Members of each individual Congress can win popularity, votes, and reelection by deficit spending to be paid for by future generations. The size of our national debt (about five trillion dollars in debt held by the public) and the persistence of deficits (in 65 of the 77 years from 1931 to 2007) show that this is a major problem that we cannot solve with normal legislation.

A Balanced Budget Amendment has been repeatedly introduced in the U.S. Congress, several times by Republican Representative Ernest J. Istook Jr. of Oklahoma (in Congress from 1993-2007) along with many other sponsors. In 1995 the amendment passed the House with an overwhelming majority of 300 votes in favor, but was one vote short of a two thirds majority in the Senate.

There are many versions of a proposed balanced budget amendment. Such proposals commonly require a three fifths majority of all the members of each house of Congress, on a roll call vote, to approve any deficit spending or increase in debt, and require the President to submit a balanced budget each year. Some versions suspend these rules in a time of war or military conflict, which seems unnecessary; if a war truly threatens us, then getting three fifths of members to vote for needed deficit spending should not be a problem. Figure 12.1 gives example language for a straightforward balanced budget amendment.

Amendment XXVIII

Section 1. Total outlays for any fiscal year shall not exceed total receipts for that fiscal year, unless three-fifths of the whole number of each House of Congress shall provide by law for a specific excess of outlays over receipts by a roll call vote.

Section 2. The limit on the debt of the United States held by the public shall not be increased, unless three-fifths of the whole number of each House of Congress shall provide by law for a specific increase by a roll call vote.

Section 3. Before each fiscal year, the President shall transmit to the Congress a proposed budget for the United States Government for that fiscal year in which total outlays do not exceed total receipts.

Section 4. Total receipts shall include all receipts of the United States Government except those derived from borrowing. Total outlays shall include all outlays of the United States Government except those for repayment of debt principal.

Section 5. The Congress shall enforce and implement this article by appropriate legislation.

Section 6. This article shall take effect at the beginning of the second fiscal year that begins after its ratification.

Figure 12.1. Example
Balanced Budget Amendment[174]

If Congress refuses to adopt a balanced budget amendment, then the states can petition for a constitutional convention to adopt such an amendment. In the 1970s and 1980s, 32 states, two short of the two thirds needed, petitioned Congress for a convention to write a balanced budget amendment.[175] Calling for a convention puts pressure on Congress to act. The 17th amendment, for direct election of senators, was only approved by Congress after many states had called for a convention. Getting Congress to act is the most straightforward way to pass an amendment.

Restore PAYGO Rules in Congress

"PAYGO" is a self-imposed rule in Congress that legislative changes cannot worsen the deficit. PAYGO requires spending increases or tax cuts to be offset by spending cuts or tax increases. Congress followed PAYGO rules from 1990 to 2002, eventually reducing the deficit and producing four years of budget surpluses from fiscal years 1998 to 2001. After the Democrats won control of Congress in the 2006 elections, the Democratic leadership reinstated PAYGO rules in the House of Representatives.[176]

Limit Earmarked Spending

Senator John McCain and several other senators have introduced a Pork-Barrel Reduction Act that would allow unauthorized spending to be challenged and then removed, unless 60 senators voted to keep such spending.

By law we should prohibit federal agencies from spending funds on earmarks included only in conference reports and not in legislation, as conference reports are not law.[177]

Publish Most Federal Spending as It Happens

"We might hope to see the finances of the Union as clear and intelligible as a merchant's books, so that every member of Congress and every man of any mind in the Union should be able to comprehend them, to investigate abuses, and consequently to control them."—President Thomas Jefferson to Treasury Secretary Albert Gallatin in 1802

The Internet provides a great opportunity to make federal spending more visible to everyone. Our government already makes its major annual financial reports freely available on the World Wide Web: the budget, trustees reports for Social Security and Medicaid, and documents from the Congressional Budget Office (CBO) and Government Accountability Office (GAO).

We may not want grandpa's Social Security check to be public knowledge, nor the detailed spending of the Central Intelligence Agency, but we should publish most federal spending down to the most detailed level. Anyone will then be able to see each subsidy check and each payment for goods and services in near real time. Sunshine is a great disinfectant. The Federal Funding Accountability and Transparency Act of 2006, already enacted, is a small first step. It creates a searchable database of federally funded projects that any citizen can access on the Internet.

Here is just one example of why our government should account in detail to the public for each dollar spent. In the summer of 2003 the U.S. government transferred more than $8 billion to Iraqi control after invading and occupying Iraq. More than $5 billion in cash was brought into Iraq by airplane, in shrink-wrapped packages of $100 bills. Most of those billions of dollars disappeared, all at taxpayer expense.[178] If government officials know that all citizens can see each and every expenditure, then perhaps they will not be so foolish.

Restore the President's Impoundment Power

"Presidents Kennedy, Johnson, and Nixon used the impoundment power routinely—and in some years used it to cut federal appropriations by more than 5 percent. In one year Richard Nixon impounded more than 7 percent of domestic appropriations."—Stephen Moore, in testimony to Congress for the Cato Institute[179]

For most of U.S. history, Presidents have had the power to not spend monies appropriated by Congress, the power of *impoundment.* President Thomas Jefferson first used the impoundment power in 1801, refusing to spend $50,000 appropriated for Navy gunboats.

Congress took the impoundment power away from Presidents in the Congressional Budget and Impoundment Control Act of 1974, during President Nixon's last year in office. Nixon was weakened by the Watergate scandal and had angered Congress by impounding so much spending; those impoundments were unrelated to Watergate. Losing the impoundment power has weakened the President's role in federal spending and increased spending by hundreds of billions of dollars since 1974.

Congress can restore the President's impoundment power through legislation and should do so immediately. The impoundment power is broader and easier to implement than the better known line item veto, which may require a constitutional amendment to adopt. (The Line Item Veto Act of 1996, used by President Clinton to veto some spending, was found unconstitutional in 1998.)

National Choices

"Drastic action may be costly, but it can be less expensive than continuing inaction."—Richard E. Neustadt in Presidential Power: The Politics of Leadership[180]

There is no soaring rhetoric to conclude this book. Its essence is unforgiving mathematics. We have these national choices available:

- Huge spending cuts, as described in this book or similar in size

- Huge tax increases

- Some combination of very large spending cuts and very large tax increases

- Putting off these painful choices for a few more years, at the cost of needing even larger spending cuts or tax increases in the future

- Perhaps putting off these choices too long and stumbling into default, hyperinflation, or a major collapse of government programs

- Perhaps doing a little of this and a little of that but not enough, creating a future of increasing debt and taxes with decreasing government programs, while never getting out of debt

Personal Choices

Each of us also has personal choices: Do I agree with the facts in this book? Do I agree with the spending cuts proposed in this book? Are there other fixes for these problems that I prefer? Will I act as a voter, blogger, journalist, campaign contributor, candidate, or community member to fix our federal budget crisis?

If it seems unlikely that we Americans will make these changes, consider how unlikely it was that a society of backwoods farmers and hillbillies could win a war against the world's largest empire, succeed at self government, and become the world's greatest nation. It happened, from 1776 to now. Let's keep it going!

A BUDGET TABLES

This appendix summarizes all of this book's proposed federal budget savings.

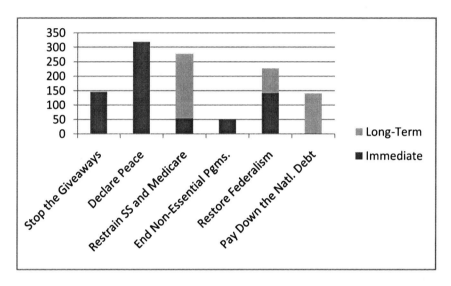

Figure A.1. This Book's Annual Budget Savings

Table A.1 shows the immediate and long-term budget savings proposed in this book, totaling more than $1.1 trillion per year. Savings from paying down the national debt depend on both adopting this book's proposals for immediate savings and not spending those savings on new programs or tax cuts.

Table A.1. Total Immediate and Long-Term Budget Savings

Major Proposal (Chapter)	Saved Each Year Immediate	Saved Each Year Long-Term
Stop the Give-Aways (6)	$145.8 billion	-
Declare Peace (7)	$319.0 billion	-
Restrain Social Security and Medicare (8)	$53.8 billion	$223.5 billion
End Non-Essential Programs (9)	$50.4 billion	-
Restore Federalism (10)	$141.2 billion	$85.9 billion
Pay Down the National Debt (11)	-	$140.0 billion
Imm. and Long-Term Savings	**$710.2 billion**	**$449.4 billion**
Grand Total Annual Savings	**$1,159.6 billion = $1.1596 trillion**	

Table A.2 shows how much we will save per person, per family, and for our country, each year for a lifetime.

Table A.2. Enact This Book's Proposed Spending Cuts Savings

	Saved Each Year	Saved in a Lifetime
Per Person	$3,865	$309,200
Per Family	$15,460	$1,236,800
For Our Country	$1,159.6 billion	$92,768 billion

Tables A.3 to A.8 show the savings from Chapters 6 to 11.

Table A.3. Budget Savings in Chapter 6
Stop the Giveaways

Proposal	Saved Each Year	Saved in a Lifetime
End Pork	$24.0 billion	$1,920 billion
End Farm Programs	$34.8 billion	$2,784 billion
Stop Subsidizing Debt	$24.0 billion	$1,920 billion
End Foreign Aid	$22.3 billion	$1,784 billion
End Long-Term Disaster Relief and Insurance	$22.3 billion	$1,784 billion
End Corporate Welfare	$9.0 billion	$720 billion
Stop Subsidizing Medical Education	$9.4 billion	$752 billion
Total Chapter 6 Immediate Savings	**$145.8 billion**	**$11,664 billion**

Table A.4. Budget Savings in Chapter 7
Declare Peace

Proposal	Saved Each Year	Saved in a Lifetime
Stop the Iraq War	$97.5 billion	$7,800 billion
End the Afghanistan War	$18.6 billion	$1,488 billion
Cut the Remaining Defense Budget by 50%	$202.9 billion	$16,232 billion
Total Chapter 7 Immediate Savings	**$319.0 billion**	**$25,520 billion**

Table A.5. Budget Savings in Chapter 8
Restrain Social Security and Medicare

Proposal	Saved Each Year	Saved in a Lifetime
Raise Social Security Retirement Ages (Long Term)	$147.2 billion	$11,776 billion
Medicare High-Deductible Higher Payments by Beneficiaries	$53.8 billion	$4,304 billion
Medicare High-Deductible Lower Spending (Long Term)	$76.3 billion	$6,104 billion
Total Chapter 8 Savings	**$277.3 billion**	**$22,184 billion**

Table A.6. Budget Savings in Chapter 9
End Non-Essential Programs

Proposal	Saved Each Year	Saved in a Lifetime
Sell NASA	$15.1 billion	$1,208 billion
Leave Art and Media to the Free Market	$0.6 billion	$48 billion
End Federal Funding for Biomedical Research	$28.2 billion	$2,256 billion
End Federal Funding for the National Science Foundation	$5.5 billion	$440 billion
Sell Amtrak	$1.0 billion	$80 billion
Total Chapter 9 Immediate Savings	**$50.4 billion**	**$4,032 billion**

Table A.7. Budget Saving in Chapter 10
Restore Federalism

Proposal	Saved Each Year	Saved in a Lifetime
End Most Federal Education Programs	$47.8 billion	$3,824 billion
End Many Grants to State and Local Governments	$93.4 billion	$7,472 billion
Make Medicaid a Block Grant (Long Term)	$85.9 billion	$6,872 billion
Total Chapter 10 Savings	**$227.1 billion**	**$18,168 billion**

Table A.8. Budget Saving in Chapter 11
Consequences

Proposal	Saved Each Year	Saved in a Lifetime
Pay Down the National Debt (Long Term)	$140.0 billion	$11,200 billion
Total Chapter 11 Savings	**$140.0 billion**	**$11,200 billion**

B RESOURCES

We are in the Internet age. These resources are accessed most easily using personal computers, the World Wide Web, electronic mail, and a high-speed Internet connection. If a resource's web address has changed since this book was published, you should be able to locate it using a search engine, like Google. Many federal documents and public policy papers are provided in Adobe Portable Document Format, as PDF files. These files are viewed with the free Adobe Reader software, available at http://www.adobe.com.

Facts about Federal Finances

The Office of Management and Budget (OMB) publishes the President's budget each year, usually early in February. At http://www.whitehouse.gov/omb/.

The Congressional Budget Office (CBO) analyzes federal finances and policy options on behalf of Congress. At http://www.cbo.gov.

The Government Accountability Office (GAO) audits federal finances, has been warning about the federal budget crisis (Fiscal Wake-Up Tour), and creates the annual Financial Report of the U.S. Government, usually in December. At http://www.gao.gov.

Other Information about the Federal Budget Crisis

The Coming Generational Storm: What You Need to Know about America's Economic Future by Laurence J. Kotlikoff and Scott Burns has much more information about the economics and demographics of the federal budget crisis, including a detailed discussion of generational equity, plus their own suggested solutions and advice for how to prepare your personal finances for the federal budget crisis.

Running on Empty: How the Democratic and Republican Parties are Bankrupting Our Future and What Americans Can Do About It by Peter G. Peterson focuses on how our political parties have gotten us into the federal budget crisis, and the kind of political reforms that we need.

There are many think tanks in the United States, non-profit organizations that analyze and report on public policy. My favorite is the Cato Institute, at http://www.cato.org. Cato provides many free publications about reducing spending and also publishes books, including *Downsizing the Federal Government* by Chris Edwards, which makes many detailed proposals for federal budget cuts, some identical to proposals in this book, such as Medicaid block grants.

The Concord Coalition is a nationwide, grass roots organization advocating generationally responsible fiscal policy. At http://www.concordcoalition.org.

Citizens Against Government Waste fights wasteful earmarks and pork spending. At http://www.cagw.org.

Elected Officials and Political Parties

The White House (President, Vice President, and their staff) is online at http://www.whitehouse.gov. The U.S. Congress is at http://www.house.gov and http://www.senate.gov. It is important to use the .gov suffix in government Internet addresses as disreputable web sites sometimes use the corresponding .com addresses.

Our two major political parties are the Democratic Party (http://www.democrats.org) and the Republican Party (http://www.gop.org). The three minor political parties that were on large numbers of state ballots in the 2004 general election are the Constitution Party (http://www.constitutionparty.com), Green Party (http://www.gp.org), and Libertarian Party (http://www.lp.org).

Buying This Book

To Save America: How to Prevent Our Coming Federal Bankruptcy is available from Amazon.com and other fine bookstores.

Contacting the Author

You can email Martin L. Buchanan at **mlb@martinlbuchanan.com** or send postal mail to:

Martin L. Buchanan
545 Broadway #31
Denver, CO 80203

C NOTES

This book uses the following major sources, each given an abbreviation used in the notes, and all available online. The FY 2008 (FY08 below) federal budget documents are online at http://www.whitehouse.gov/omb/budget/fy2008/.

CBO07   *CBO Budget Options February 2007*, Congressional Budget Office, http://www.cbo.gov/ftpdocs/78xx/ doc7821/02-23-BudgetOptions.pdf.

FY08AP   *Analytical Perspectives, Budget of the United States Government, Fiscal Year 2008.*

FY08BUD   *The Budget for Fiscal Year 2008.*

FY08HI   *Historical Tables, Budget of the United States Government, Fiscal Year 2008.*

MC07   *The 2007 Annual Report of the Boards of Trustees of the Federal Hospital Insurance and Federal Supplementary Medical Insurance Trust Funds* (Medicare trustees' report), http://www.cms.hhs.gov/ ReportsTrustFunds/downloads/tr2007.pdf.

PORK   *All About Pork: The Abuse of Earmarks and the Needed Reforms*, May 3, 2006 report by Tom Finnigan, for Citizens Against Government Waste, http://www.cagw.org/ site/DocServer/PorkFinal.pdf.

SS07   *The 2007 Annual Report of the Board of*
        Trustees of the Federal Old-Age and Survivors
        Insurance and Federal Disability Insurance
        Trust Funds (Social Security trustees' report),
        http://www.ssa.gov/OACT/TR/TR07/tr07.pdf.

STATAB07 *Statistical Abstract of the United States 2007*,
        U.S. Census Bureau, http://www.census.gov/
        prod/2006pubs/07statab.

References beginning with http:// are addresses (URLs) of
documents on the Internet's World Wide Web.

Notes for Chapter 1, Introduction

[1] "Long-Term Budget Outlook: Deficits Matter—Saving Our Future
Requires Tough Choices Today," Statement of David M. Walker
Comptroller General of the United States, January 23, 2007, Testimony
Before the Committee on the Budget, House of Representatives,
GAO-07-389T, Page 12.

[2] This book generally uses figures for fiscal year 2006 (FY 2006), the last
year for which complete data was available. The FY 2006 federal deficit
was $248 billion. The projected deficit for FY 2007 is lower, $205 billion.

[3] "The Nation's Long-Term Fiscal Outlook: April 2007 Update"
GAO-07-983R, page 8, http://www.gao.gov/new.items/d07983r.pdf
calculates the fiscal gap for current policies (the *alternative* projection)
as 7.4% of GDP or .074 x $13,061.1 billion = $966.5 billion per year,
nearly $1 trillion per year in FY 2006.

Notes for Chapter 2, Understanding the Federal Budget

4 http://www.taxfoundation.org/taxfreedomday/.

5 FY08HI, Table 3.2, Outlays by Function and Subfunction: 1962-2012, page 72.

6 FY08HI, Table 10.1, Gross Domestic Product and Deflators Used in the Historical Tables: 1940-2012, page 193.

7 FY08HI, Table 3-1, Outlays by Superfunction and Function, page 54, provides values for national defense and veterans spending, Medicare spending, and net interest. Medicaid and related (State Children's Health Insurance Program, SCHIP) spending for FY 2006 is from FY08BUD, Department of Health and Human Services, page 73. Old age and survivors Social Security payments for FY 2006 are estimated by taking 25% of OASI payments for calendar year 2005 and 75% of OASI payments for calendar year 2006, from the Social Security Administration's actuarial publication, "Social Security and Medicare Benefits," updated Feb 9, 2007, http://www.ssa.gov/OACT/STATS/table4a4.html.

8 FY08HI, Table 1.1—Summary of Receipts, Outlays, and Surpluses or Deficits (-): 1789-2012, page 22.

9 FY08HI, Table 1.2—Summary of Receipts, Outlays, and Surpluses or Deficits (-) as Percentages of GDP: 1930-2012, pp. 23-24.

Notes for Chapter 3, Understanding Federal Debt and Deficits

10 SS07, page 4. The 2006 ending balance for the OASDI trust funds was more than $2 trillion.

11 *A Free Nation Deep in Debt: The Financial Roots of Democracy* by James MacDonald, pp. 292-306, 361, 401-402.

[12] FY08HI, Table 1.1, Summary of Receipts, Outlays, and Surpluses or Deficits: 1789-2012, page 22.

[13] Republicans controlled both houses of Congress for two years from January 1947 to January 1949, overlapping the time during which the 1947 to 1949 federal budgets were determined, but not an exact match.

[14] "Mr. Bush's Deficit Dance" in The Washington Post, Tue Feb 6, 2007 page A-16, http://www.washingtonpost.com/ wp-dyn/content/article/2007/02/05/AR2007020501289.html.

[15] SS07, page 3.

[16] http://www.concordcoalition.org/issues/feddebt/debt-facts.html for the overall facts on foreign holdings of federal debt, as of July 6, 2006.

[17] http://www.ustreas.gov/tic/mfh.txt. Japan holds more than $600 billion in federal debt, but another U.S.-Japan conflict is unlikely.

[18] http://en.wikipedia.org/wiki/U.S._public_debt.

[19] Schedule of Federal Debt ... through February 28, 2007, http://www.treasurydirect.gov/govt/reports/ pd/feddebt/feddebt_feb07.pdf.

[20] http://www.federalreserve.gov/boardDocs/speeches/ 2001/20010427/default.htm.

[21] FY08HI, Table 7.1. Federal Debt at the End of Year: 1940-2012, pp. 126-127.

Notes for Chapter 4, The Federal Budget Crisis

[22] There are still 77 million living Baby Boomers born in the United States from 1946 to 1964. The Census Bureau figures include immigrants of the same age and cover a 20-year span rather than a 19-year span of ages, for more than 82 million people.

23 STATAB07, Table 11, Resident Population by Age and Sex: 1980 to 2005, page 12.

24 http://en.wikipedia.org/wiki/Demography_of_the_United_States has a good table of fertility: 1950=3.69, 1960=3.76, 1970=2.48, 1980=1.81, 1990=1.90,2000=2.01, 2007 (estimated)=2.09.

25 STATAB07, Table 12, Resident Population Projections by Sex and Age: 2010 to 2050, page 13.

26 MC07, Table II.C.1, Ultimate Assumptions, page 7. The trustees assume that Medicare real spending per beneficiary grows at the rate of real GDP growth + one percentage point, or 2.5% per year assuming real GDP growth of 1.5% per year.

27 *The Diagnosis and Treatment of Medicare* by Andrew J. Rettenmaier and Thomas R. Saving, published by the American Enterprise Institute, Table 2-1 on page 28, drawn from the *2004 Review of Assumptions and Methods of the Medicare Trustees' Financial Projections*.

28 *The Diagnosis and Treatment of Medicare* by Andrew J. Rettenmaier and Thomas R. Saving, published by the American Enterprise Institute, page 8.

29 STATAB07, Table 11, Resident Population by Age and Sex: 1980 to 2005, page 12.

30 http://www.gao.gov/special.pubs/longterm/ april2007altsimulation.txt.

31 http://www.gao.gov/special.pubs/longterm/ april2007baseline_tabdelimited.txt.

32 Long-Term Budget Outlook, Deficits Matter—Saving Our Future Requires Tough Choices Today, Testimony Before the Committee on the Budget, House of Representatives, Statement of David M. Walker,

Comptroller General of the United States, January 23, 2007, GAO-07-389T.

33 CIA World Factbook's rank order table of public debt at https://www.cia.gov/cia/publications/factbook/rankorder/ 2186rank.html. Japan, with debt of 176% of GDP is the only advanced nation with a debt level greater than 110% of GDP. Japan's economy was stagnant for many years, partly because of its high debt levels.

34 FY08HI, Table 1-2. Summary of Receipts, Outlays, and Surpluses or Deficits (-) As Percentages of GDP: 1930-2012, pp. 23-24.

35 SS07, page 8.

36 MC07, page 4.

37 GAO's April 2007 alternative simulation data from http://www.gao.gov/special.pubs/longterm/april2007altsimulation.txt.

Notes for Chapter 5, Federal Bankruptcy

38 http://www.gao.gov/special.pubs/longterm/tourqa.html, Tour Q&A for the Fiscal Wake-Up Tour.

39 http://www.diploweb.com/english/russia/laughland1.htm.

40 *A Free Nation Deep in Debt: The Financial Roots of Democracy* by James MacDonald, pages 130, 144, and 360.

41 http://en.wikipedia.org/wiki/Argentine_debt_restructuring.

42 http://en.wikipedia.org/wiki/Argentina.

43 http://en.wikipedia.org/wiki/Hyperinflation for hyperinflation episodes and https://www.cia.gov/cia/publications/factbook/ rankorder/2001rank.html for ranking of national economies.

44 http://facweb.furman.edu/~dstanford/a43/a43chapter2.htm.

45 https://www.cia.gov/cia/publications/factbook/rankorder/2004rank.html for ranking of per-capita GDP.

46 "The Right and Wrong Ways to Reform Pensions in Russia" by Laurence J.Kotlikoff, Professor of Economics at Boston University, http://www.bu.edu/econ/workingpapers/papers/Laurence%20J.%20Kotlikoff/RussianPensionReform.pdf.

47 http://www.epn-magazine.com/news/fullstory.php/aid/2766/In_brief.html, European Pensions & Investment News, 21 May 2007.

48 http://www.pbs.org/wgbh/pages/frontline/shows/russia/readings/fears.html.

49 *Helvering* v. *Davis*, 301 U.S.609, at 619, and *Flemming* v. *Nestor*, 363 U.S. 603, at 616. Both cited in *Social Security: The Inherent Contradiction* by Peter J. Ferrara, 1980 from the Cato Institute, p. 70.

50 SS07, page 8. There is significant uncertainty when projecting so far into the future. The trustees use three sets of assumptions for forecasting: intermediate, high-cost, and low-cost. The 2041 date is for the intermediate (most likely) assumptions. Using the high-cost assumptions, Social Security exhausts its trust fund in 2031. Using the low-cost assumptions, Social Security never exhausts its trust fund for the next 75 years (see page 15 for a comparison of the three projections).

51 "Drifting to Future Bankruptcy" by Laurence J. Kotlikoff, in *The Philadelphia Inquirer*, 10/22/2006.

52 FY08HI, Table 1-2. Summary of Receipts, Outlays, and Surpluses or Deficits (-) As Percentages of GDP: 1930-2012, pp. 23-24. 50 out of 61 years from 1946 to 2006 show receipts in a range of 17-20% of GDP.

53 A 1.6% of GDP federal tax increase times FY 2006 GDP of $13,061.1 billion equals $209 billion per year in more revenue, about 20% of the fiscal gap.

54 http://en.wikipedia.org/wiki/Government_shutdown.

55 http://en.wikipedia.org/wiki/Balance_of_trade#
United_States_trade_deficit.

56 *2006 Financial Report of the U.S. Government*, pp. 41-43.

57 "Long-Term Budget Outlook: Deficits Matter—Saving Our Future
Requires Tough Choices Today," Statement of David M. Walker
Comptroller General of the United States, January 23, 2007, Testimony
Before the Committee on the Budget, House of Representatives,
GAO-07-389T, Page 12.

58 "The Nation's Long-Term Fiscal Outlook: April 2007 Update"
GAO-07-983R, page 8, http://www.gao.gov/new.items/d07983r.pdf.

59 *The Coming Generational Storm: What You Need to Know about
America's Economic Future* by Laurence J. Kotlikoff and Scott Burns,
p. 65 of the trade paperback edition.

Notes for Chapter 6, Stop the Giveaways

60 Earmarks in Appropriations Acts, http://www.fas.org/sgp/crs/
misc/m012606.pdf, January 26, 2006 memorandum by the
Congressional Research Service (CRS) appropriations team (found via
http://en.wikipedia.org/wiki/Earmarking). The author excluded from
the CRS figures the listed earmarks for "Foreign Operations, Export
Financing, and Related Program's Appropriations" as those earmarks
include routine annual designations of billions of dollars in foreign aid
for specific countries, such as Egypt and Israel. Excluding that category
leaves 15,623 earmarks totaling $36,893.25 billion dollars for FY 2005.

61 PORK, p.9.

62 PORK, pp. 15-16.

63 http://web.mit.edu/osp/www/earmarks.htm.

64 PORK, pp. 10-12.

65 The 2006 Pig Book from Citizens Against Government Waste (http://www.cagw.org) identifies $29 billion in pork for 2006. This figure is multiplied by 83% to eliminate overlap with other program cuts recommended in this book, producing savings of $24 billion.

66 In the OMB earmark database for FY2005, about 17% of the earmarked amounts are in the Department of Agriculture, Department of Commerce, Department of Education, Department of Energy, Department of Housing and Urban Development, International Assistance Programs, NASA, or the Small Business Administration, programs cut elsewhere in this book. http://www.whitehouse.gov/omb/earmarks/preview-public-site/agencies742a.html?source=APP.

67 http://etext.virginia.edu/jefferson/quotations/jeff1320.htm.

68 "Can America's farmers be weaned from their government money?" The Economist September 7, 2006. (Internet access to this article requires a subscription.)

69 "Farm Program Pays $1.3 Billion to People Who Don't Farm," by Dan Morgan, Gilbert M. Gaul and Sarah Cohen, The Washington Post, Sunday July 2, 2006 (http://www.washingtonpost.com/wp-dyn/content/article/2006/07/01/AR2006070100962_pf.html.

70 "Liberalizing Agriculture: Why the United States Should Look to New Zealand and Australia," Policy Backgrounder #1624, February 19, 2003, from the Heritage Foundation, http://www.heritage.org/Research/Agriculture/bg1624.cfm. Sugar is not the healthiest part of the U.S. diet, but sugar prices should not be increased to support special interests.

71 "Six Reasons to Kill Farm Subsidies and Trade Barriers" by Daniel Griswold, Stephen Slivinski, and Christopher Preble, February 2006, http://www.reason.com/0602/fe.dg.six.shtml.

[72] "Farm Subsidies: Devastating the World's Poor and the Environment" by Max Borders and H. Sterling Burnett, Brief Analysis No. 547, March 24, 2006, National Center for Policy Analysis.

[73] "Six Reasons to Kill Farm Subsidies and Trade Barriers" by Daniel Griswold, Stephen Slivinski, and Christopher Preble, February 2006, http://www.reason.com/0602/fe.dg.six.shtml.

[74] "Six Reasons to Kill Farm Subsidies and Trade Barriers" by Daniel Griswold, Stephen Slivinski, and Christopher Preble, February 2006, http://www.reason.com/0602/fe.dg.six.shtml.

[75] "Liberalizing Agriculture: Why the United States Should Look to New Zealand and Australia," Policy Backgrounder #1624, February 19, 2003, from the Heritage Foundation, http://www.heritage.org/Research/ Agriculture/bg1624.cfm.

[76] FY08BUD, Department of Agriculture, page 34 lists FY 2006 actual spending.

[77] FY08AP, Chapter 7, "Credit and Insurance," Table 7-1, Estimated Future Cost of Outstanding Federal Credit Programs, pp. 87-88, lists the totals for outstanding direct loans and loan guarantees.

[78] http://www.citizen.org/pressroom/release.cfm?ID=1960.

[79] FY08AP, Chapter 7, "Credit and Insurance," pp. 70-72 describes government's role in providing FHA and VA mortgages with low or no down payments.

[80] "Making College More Expensive: The Unintended Consequence of Federal Tuition Aid" by Gary Wolfram, Cato Institute Policy Analysis #531, January 25, 2005, http://www.cato.org/pubs/pas/pa531.pdf.

[81] FY08AP, Chapter 7, "Credit and Insurance," Table 7-1, Estimated Future Cost of Outstanding Federal Credit Programs, pp. 87-88, shows

those estimated future costs increasing from $89 billion to $113 billion or by $24 billion during FY 2006.

82 http://en.wikipedia.org/wiki/Israel-United_States_relations #United_States_military_and_economic_aid.

83 http://en.wikipedia.org/wiki/Palestinian_Authority #Foreign_aid_and_budget_deficit.

84 http://en.wikipedia.org/wiki/Hamas.

85 One of the most notorious aid grants tied to anti-drug efforts in other countries was a grant of $43 million to the Taliban government of Afghanistan in May 2001, less than four months before Osama bin Laden, allied with that government, attacked the United States. See "How Washington Funded the Taliban" by Ted Galen Carpenter, http://www.cato.org/pub_display.php?pub_id=3556.

86 *The White Man's Burden: Why the West's Efforts to Aid the Rest Have Done So Much Ill and So Little Good* by William Easterly.

87 http://en.wikipedia.org/wiki/People%27s_Republic_of_China #Economy.

88 http://www.charitynavigator.org/index.cfm/bay/ search.summary/orgid/3499.htm. The author has supported CCF for many years and currently sponsors two children in India.

89 http://www.charitynavigator.org.

90 FY08BUD, Department of State and Other International Programs, page 105. Eliminating all spending items except for Diplomatic and Consular Programs; Embassy Security, Construction, and Maintenance; International Peacekeeping; and International Organizations saves $22,305 million ($22.3 billion) from FY 2006 actual spending.

[91] "President Bush continues to follow through with the Federal commitment to do what it takes to help residents of the Gulf Coast rebuild their lives in the wake of this disaster, with $110.6 billion in Federal aid alone going towards relief, recovery and rebuilding efforts." From "Hurricane Katrina: What Government is Doing" at the Department of Homeland Security web site, at http://www.dhs.gov/xprepresp/programs/gc_1157649340100.shtm.

[92] FY08AP, Chapter 7, "Credit and Insurance," pp. 83-84.

[93] FY08BUD, Department of Homeland Security, page 80, total of FEMA discretionary and mandatory spending.

[94] http://en.thinkexist.com/quotation/government-help-to_business_is_just_as_disastrous/222074.html.

[95] *Downsizing the Federal Government* by Chris Edwards, page 169.

[96] *Downsizing the Federal Government* by Chris Edwards, page 90.

[97] FY08BUD, Small Business Administration discretionary spending of $1,472 million in FY 2006 (page 142), Department of Energy spending on Energy Resources and Science totaling $6,697 million (page 61), and Department of Commerce spending on four programs totaling $787 million (page 40). All totaling $8,956 million or $9.0 billion.

[98] CBO07, Option 550-14 on page 163. In 1960 there were 142 physicians per 100,000 people; in 2000 there were 288 physicians per 100,000 people.

[99] CBO07, Options 550-14 ($150 million), 570-3 ($665 million, based on FY2007 value of $700 million reduced 5%), 570-5 ($2,300 million), 570-6 ($5,959 million, based on FY2008 value of $6,621 million which is calculated from a 58.9% cut in subsidies saving $3,900 million and this proposal is for a 100% cut in subsidies), and 570-7 ($360 million, based on FY 2008 value of $700 million reduced 10%). Totaling $9,434 million estimated FY 2006 value for savings.

Notes for Chapter 7, Declare Peace

[100] http://www.edchange.org/multicultural/speeches/ ike_chance_for_peace.html.

[101] Military spending except Russia per The CIA World Factbook rank order table at https://www.cia.gov/cia/publications/factbook/ rankorder/2067rank.html. http://www.globalsecurity.org/military/ world/spending.htm estimates Russia's military spending as $50 billion per year.

[102] WorldPublicOpinion.org survey carried out September 1-4, 2006 by the Program on International Policy Attitudes (PIPA) at the University of Maryland is the source of all poll results.

[103] "The Cost of Iraq, Afghanistan, and Other Global War on Terror Operations Since 9/11" Updated March 14, 2007, Congressional Research Service (CRS) Order Code RL33110, page CRS-8 lists $97.5 billion in budget authority (not outlays). Page CRS-23 estimates an Iraq DOD spending rate in early FY 2006 of $8.6 billion per month, or $103.2 billion per year. http://fpc.state.gov/documents/organization/ 82502.pdf.

[104] http://en.wikiquote.org/wiki/David_Ben-Gurion.

[105] http://www.ynetnews.com/articles/0,7340,L-3255291,00.html. FY2007 appropriations include $2.4 billion for Israel and $1.7 billion for Egypt.

[106] The United States was already allied with Israel at the time of the Yom Kippur War, and our aid to Israel in that war was both moral and proper because of that existing alliance. This book suggests that alliances with Israel, Taiwan, and other countries embroiled in civil wars is bad policy and that we should end such alliances, which would end our involvement in such wars in the future.

107 http://en.wikipedia.org/wiki/
International_Security_Assistance_Force.

108 "Afghanistan: Narcotics and U.S. Policy" updated December 10,
2006, Congressional Research Service (CRS) Order Code RL32686.
http://fpc.state.gov/documents/organization/79345.pdf. Page CRS-3
gives key facts: 6,100 metric tons of opium with a value of over $3 billion,
which is 45% of the country's GDP from legitimate sources, directly
supporting 2.9 million Afghans. One discrepancy is that this is described
as 12.6% of the Afghan population, while the CIA World Factbook gives
the Afghan population as over 31 million, implying that the correct figure
is about 9.3% (2.9/31.1). Any statistics about illegal activities in any
country are imprecise, including these statistics.

109 The CIA World Factbook entry for Afghanistan:
https://www.cia.gov/cia/publications/factbook/geos/af.html.

110 "The Cost of Iraq, Afghanistan, and Other Global War on Terror
Operations Since 9/11" Updated March 14, 2007, Congressional Research
Service (CRS) Order Code RL33110, page CRS-8 lists $18.6 billion in
budget authority (not outlays). Page CRS-23 estimates an Operation
Enduring Freedom DOD spending rate in early FY 2006 of $1.4 billion
per month, or $16.8 billion per year. http://fpc.state.gov/documents/
organization/82502.pdf.

111 http://en.wikiquote.org/wiki/Lincoln.

112 Military spending except Russia per The CIA World Factbook rank
order table at https://www.cia.gov/cia/publications/factbook/
rankorder/2067rank.html. http://www.globalsecurity.org/military/
world/spending.htm estimates Russia's military spending as $50 billion
per year.

113 Per The CIA World Factbook rank order table at https://www.cia.gov/
cia/publications/factbook/rankorder/2067rank.html and adding Russia
between China and France in spending. U.S. allies: France, Japan, United
Kingdom, Germany, Italy, South Korea, Australia, Turkey, Spain,

Canada, Israel, Mexico, and Greece. Friendly to the U.S.: India, Saudi Arabia, Brazil, and Taiwan. Neither allies nor enemies: China and Russia.

[114] http://www.globalsecurity.org/wmd/library/news/iran/2006/ iran-060531-irna03.htm from 5/31/2006, citing 2005 figures from the International Institute for Strategic Studies in London.

[115] FY08HI, Table 3-2, Outlays by Function and Subfunction: 1962-2012, on page 60 gives FY 2006 National Defense spending as $521,840 million ($521.8 billion). Subtracting $97.5 billion spent on the Iraq War and $18.6 billion spent on the Afghanistan War leaves $405.7 billion. Saving 50% of that will save $202.9 billion (rounding up).

Notes for Chapter 8, Restrain Social Security and Medicare

[116] FY08HI, Table 1-1, Summary of Receipts, Outlays, and Surpluses or Deficits (-): 1789-2012. Almost all of the off-budget surplus for FY 2006 is from Social Security taxes. Table 13-1, Cash Income, Outgo, and Balances of the Social Security and Medicare Trust Funds: 1936-2012 provides much more detail, a $176.6 billion surplus in the OASI trust fund and an $8.6 billion surplus in the DI trust fund, totaling $185.2 billion.

[117] SS07, Table IV.A1, Operations of the OASI Trust Fund, Calendar Years 2001-15 on page 33.

[118] *2006 Financial Report of the U.S. Government*, page 114. http://www.gao.gov/financial/FY 2006/fy06finanicalrpt.pdf.

[119] SS07, Overview on page 8 for both the 2041 date and the 75% figure.

[120] http://en.wikipedia.org/wiki/Elsie_McLean.

[121] SS07, pp. 9-10.

[122] "Raising the Retirement Age for Social Security," Issue Brief, American Academy of Actuaries, October 2002. http://www.actuary.org/pdf/socialsecurity/age_oct02.pdf, page 2.

[123] Email communication from Ron Gebhardtsbauer, FSA, EA, MAAA, FCA, MSPA and Senior Pension Fellow at the American Academy of Actuaries on April 3, 2007, excerpts of key points: "We don't have any models at the Academy for pricing SS proposals. ... That said, I can tell you that your proposal would probably solve about 100% of the financial problem because it is what I call the FAST increase in retirement ages. ... A 2% of payroll fix is approximately what is needed for a 100% fix for the 75-year window (SLOW indexation of SS NRA thereafter would keep SS in good shape)."

[124] SS07 shows the 75-year actuarial balance under intermediate assumptions (2007-81) in Table IV.B5 on page 58. The present value of the 75-year actuarial deficit, on January 1, 2007, is $5,076 billion. That is, if we had 5 trillion in the bank on January 1, 2007 in addition to expected tax revenues, then Social Security could pay its bills for the next 75 years and maintain a modest reserve (enough to pay one year of benefits) through the end of that period. The long-term real interest rate assumption of 2.9% used by the intermediate assumptions produces an annualized value of 2.9% of $5,076 billion = $147.2 billion.

[125] "Social Security: Wage Indexing Vs. Price Indexing Initial Benefits" National Committee to Preserve Social Security and Medicare http://www.ncpssm.org/news/archive/vp_wageindex/.

[126] http://en.wikipedia.org/wiki/Social_Security_%28 United_States%29#Primary_insurance_amount. The Social Security PIA (primary insurance amount) used to determine a retirement benefit is 90% of AIME (average indexed monthly earnings) below the first bend point in the formula, plus 32% of AIME between the two bend points, plus 15% of AIME above the second bend point. So for each added dollar of average earnings a low-income worker has 90 cents added to the primary benefit amount and a high-income worker has 15 cents added to the primary benefit amount, one sixth as much.

[127] *Social Security and Its Discontents: Perspectives on Choice*, edited by Michael D. Tanner. Available from http://www.cato.org.

[128] MC07, page 166, Table V.B1, average per beneficiary costs will exceed $13,000 for the period 2007 to 2016 (increasing from over $10,000 to over $16,000 per beneficiary).

[129] American Academy of Actuaries Issue Brief, "Medicare's Financial Condition: Beyond Actuarial Balance," May 2006. See Table 1, HI Income Shortfall and SMI General Revenue Contribution, on page 4. http://www.actuary.org/pdf/medicare/trustees_may06.pdf.

[130] MC07, page 30, Table III.A1, "Total Medicare Income, Expenditures, and Trust Fund Assets during Calendar Years 1970-2016."

[131] "Medicare Drug Benefit May Cost $1.2 Trillion" by Gene Connolly and Mike Allen, Washington Post, February 9, 2005, page A01. http://www.washingtonpost.com/wp-dyn/articles/ A9328-2005Feb8.html. While the gross cost given is $1.2 trillion, related offsets and savings reduce costs to $720 billion. The article also includes estimated annual Part D costs for 2014 and 2015 and a description of the threat to fire Medicare's chief actuary when the legislation was originally considered.

[132] "The Cost of Coverage" by Amy Finkelstein, in the Wall Street Journal of February 28, 2007. Ms. Finkelstein is an assistant professor of economics at MIT. By 1970, Medicare had already caused a 37% increase in hospital spending.

[133] "The Cost of Coverage" by Amy Finkelstein, in the Wall Street Journal of February 28, 2007. Ms. Finkelstein is an assistant professor of economics at MIT. "If I extrapolate from the Medicare experience to compute the effect of the overall spread of insurance—both public and private—between 1950 and 1990, it suggests that it is responsible for about half of the six-fold growth in real per capita health-care spending during this period."

[134] *Medicare Meets Mephistopheles* by David A. Hyman, published by the Cato Institute in 2006, page 18. Medicare processes more than one billion fee-for-service claims each year. One billion divided by about 43 million Medicare enrollees in 2006 equals more than 23 claims annually per beneficiary.

[135] Existing income data reported to the IRS or known to the Social Security Administration would provide most of the needed income information, though it could be two months into the year before final deductible amounts are determined. Basing deductibles on beneficiary income also creates new incentives for shifting income, perhaps to other family members, just as families have often shifted assets to shelter them from Medicaid and qualify seniors for Medicaid-paid nursing home care.

[136] http://www.cepr.net/publications/medicare_waste_2006_07.pdf.

[137] http://pubdb3.census.gov/macro/032006/hhinc/new02_001.htm, U.S. Census Bureau, Current Population Survey, 2006 Social and Economic Supplement.

[138] http://aspe.hhs.gov/poverty/06poverty.shtml, 2006 Federal Poverty Guidelines, U.S. Department of Health and Human Services.

[139] "Consumer-Directed Health Plans: Potential Effects on Health Care Spending and Outcomes," December 2006 from the Congressional Budget Office, gives some support for the 5% figure, but the studies cited are for non-elderly populations. On the other hand, the isolated experiments and individual plans cited in that study don't benefit from the global downward pressure on demand and costs caused by switching everyone in Medicare to a high-deductible plan, so 5% seems reasonable. http://www.cbo.gov/ftpdocs/77xx/doc7700/12-21-HealthPlans.pdf.

[140] MC07, Table V.E2, Present Values of Projected Revenue and Cost Components of 75-Year Open-Group Obligations for HI, SMI, and OASDI on page 189, shows that Medicare (HI and SMI) expenditures for the next 75 years have a present value of $52.6 trillion. Saving 5% of that amount has a present value of $2,630 billion. Using the report's real interest rate of 2.9% produces an annualized value of $76.3 billion.

[141] http://www.cbo.gov/showdoc.cfm?index=4066&sequence=18 Congressional Budget Office, Budget Options, March 2003, section 19 of 20. Chapter 4, "Slowing the Long-Term Growth of Social Security and Medicare." This option does not include the costs of HSA subsidies to encourage delaying Medicare, but also does not envision increasing the retirement age as much as this book does.

Notes for Chapter 9, End Non-Essential Programs

[142] http://en.wikipedia.org/wiki/Aron_Ralston. Aron wrote a book, *Between A Rock And A Hard Place*, about his experience.

[143] For example, the New Horizons space probe arrives at Pluto in the year 2015 and may continue to produce useful data after that year. http://en.wikipedia.org/wiki/New_horizons.

[144] FY08BUD, National Aeronautics and Space Administration, page 133 lists FY 2006 actual spending.

[145] Financial figures from the three web sites. In some cases FY 2005 or FY 2007 figures were all that was found.

[146] http://www.nih.gov/about/budget.htm.

[147] http://en.wikipedia.org/wiki/NIH. With NIH providing 28% of biomedical research funding, 72%, $72 billion, comes from other sources.

[148] http://www.brookings.edu/FP/PROJECTS/NUCWCOST/ MANHATTN.HTM estimates spending on the World War II Manhattan Project, which developed the atomic bomb, at $20 billion measured in 1996 dollars. Consumer prices (CPI-U) increased by about 29% from 1996 to 2006, so the Manhattan Project cost about $25.8 billion in 2006 dollars, still less than one year of NIH spending.

[149] http://en.wikipedia.org/wiki/NIH. With NIH providing 28% of biomedical research funding, 72%, $72 billion, comes from other sources.

[150] FY08BUD, Department of Health and Human Services, page 72 lists FY 2006 actual spending for NIH as $28,242 million.

[151] FY08BUD, National Science Foundation, page 136, indicates that the FY 2008 budget for Networking and Information Technology is $994 million; FY 2006 value is not given. IT R&D spending for the top 81 companies from "I.T.'s Top 81 R&D Spenders," April 17, 2007 by Robert Hertzberg, Baseline, published in CIO Insight, http://www.cioinsight.com/print_article2/0,1217,a=205581,00.asp.

[152] FY08BUD, National Science Foundation, page 138 lists FY 2006 actual spending.

[153] FY08BUD, Department of Transportation, page 109.

[154] FY08BUD, Department of Transportation, pp. 109-110 indicates FY 2006 subsidies for Amtrak as $490 million for operating subsidies and $500 million for capital subsidies.

Notes for Chapter 10, Restore Federalism

[155] http://en.wikipedia.org/wiki/
Comparison_between_U.S._states_and_countries_by_GDP_
%28PPP%29 provides a comparison of economic output between U.S. states and various nations (purchasing power parity basis). Population numbers for states and countries are available from Wikipedia and many other sources.

[156] American Federation of Teachers Resolution on Fair Funding for Federal Special Education Mandates: "Whereas, special education federal mandates cost $42 billion last year;" This resolution was passed in 2000; costs are likely much higher by now. http://www.aft.org/about/resolutions/2000/funding.htm.

[157] FY08BUD, Department of Education, pp. 54-55. About $28 billion in spending is clearly for K-12 education, about $13.8 billion is clearly for college education, and the remaining $6 billion is uncertain.

[158] STATAB07, U.S. Census Bureau, Table 205, "School Expenditures ..." on page 137. http://www.census.gov/prod/2006pubs/07statab/educ.pdf.

[159] FY08BUD, Department of Education, pp. 54-55, total FY 2006 outlays of $93,447 million minus loan outlays of $32,565 million (cut elsewhere) minus Pell Grants spending of $13,045 million (kept) equals cuts of $47,837 million.

[160] STATAB07, U.S. Census Bureau, Table 424. State and Local Governments—Summary of Finances: 1990 to 2003 shows $389 billion received from the federal government and total expenditures of $2.16 trillion, or federal revenues as 18% of state and local government spending. Medicaid spending has grown rapidly in the years since, so the percentage may be increasing. http://www.census.gov/prod/2006pubs/07statab/stlocgov.pdf, page 271.

[161] Based on FY08AP, Table 8-4. Federal Grants to State and Local Governments, pp. 110-117.

[162] FYo8BUD, Department of Health and Human Services, page 68 re. number of beneficiaries and page 73 re. FY 2006 outlays.

[163] *The Cure: How Capitalism Can Save American Health Care* by Dr. David Gratzer, page 104, citing spending data from the Centers for Medicare and Medicaid Services.

[164] Federal medical assistance percentages for FY 2006, http://aspe.hhs.gov/health/fmap06.pdf. $1.33 of federal spending per dollar of state spending is based on federal Medicaid/SCHIP spending equal to 57% of total Medicaid/SCHIP spending.

[165] CBO07. Inferred from option 550-7, "Reduce the Taxes That States Are Allowed to Levy on Medicaid Providers," on page 154.

[166] http://www.milbank.org/quarterly/8301feature.pdf.

[167] Calculations by the author based on CBO and GAO projections of Medicaid spending. Per Cato Handbook on Policy 6th Edition, page 193: "According to Congressional Budget Office projections, freezing Medicaid at 2005 levels would produce $749 billion in savings by 2014," a similar estimate of savings, as estimated savings increase with time.

Notes for Chapter 11, Consequences

[168] Based on the chart on page 8 in the *2006 Financial Report of the U.S. Government*, http://www.gao.gov/financial/fy2006/ fyo6finanicalrpt.pdf. The author added the Corporation for Public Broadcasting to the list and replaced the National Foundation on the Arts and the Humanities (a term used in the 1965 enabling legislation) with the three substantive grant-making organizations created by that legislation: Institute of Museum and Library Services, National Endowment for the Arts, and National Endowment for the Humanities.

[169] Spreadsheet constructed by the author, using projected GDP values through 2012 from FYo8HI and projecting nominal GDP for each subsequent year as 5% greater, plus savings phased in as described.

Notes for Chapter 12, What is to be Done?

170 The title "What is to be Done?" was previously used by the Communist leader Vladimir Lenin for a 1902 pamphlet. I doubt that any reader of this book will confuse its contents with communism.

171 From *The Official Rules* compiled by Paul Dickson, cited in *Random House Webster's Quotationary* by Leonard Roy Frank.

172 There are also five special delegates in the U.S. House of Representatives, who vote only when the House is meeting as a Committee of the Whole and when their votes are not the deciding votes.

173 Both procedures are in Article V of the Constitution of the United States of America. Because a new Constitutional Convention has never been convened, there are legitimate questions regarding whether the states calling a convention could limit it to a single subject, such as proposing a Balanced Budget Amendment.

174 The example amendment text uses much of the text from House Joint Resolution 58 in May 2006, while dropping exceptions for declared war and certain military conflicts, dropping a new restriction on bills that raise revenue, and otherwise simplifying and cleaning up some language. HJR58 is online at http://thomas.loc.gov/cgi-bin/query/z?c109:H.J.RES.58.IH.

175 http://www.cqpress.com/incontext/constitution/docs/constitutional_amend.html.

176 http://www.washingtonpost.com/wp-dyn/content/article/2007/01/05/AR2007010500681.html.

177 PORK, p. 21.

178 "Iraq: Follow the Money" by Joy Gordon, 4/9/2007, http://www.middle-east-online.com/english/?id=20314.

[179] "Testimony of Stephen Moore, Director of Fiscal Policy Studies, The Cato Institute, before the Committee on Judiciary, U.S. House of Representatives, The Line Item Veto, March 23, 2000," http://www.cato.org/testimony/ct-smo32300.html.

[180] *Random House Webster's Quotationary* by Leonard Roy Frank, p. 5.

INDEX

956494